Mastering Math through Magic

* * * * * * * * * *

Mary A. Lombardo

A Publication of Linworth Learning

Linworth Publishing, Inc.
Worthington, Ohio

Library of Congress Cataloging-in-Publication Data

Lombardo, Mary A.
    Mastering math through magic / by Mary A. Lombardo.
        p. cm.
    Includes bibliographical references and index.
    ISBN 1-58683-124-0
    1. Magic tricks in mathematics education. 2. Mathematics--Study and teaching
(Elementary) I. Title.

QA20.M33 L66 2002
372.7--dc21

                                                                              2002032442

Published by Linworth Publishing, Inc.
480 East Wilson Bridge Road, Suite L
Worthington, Ohio 43085

ISBN: 978-1-58683-124-0

5 4 3 2 1

Table of Contents

✳ ✳ ✳ ✳ ✳ ✳ ✳ ✳ ✳ ✳ ✳

About the Author

✳ ✳ ✳ ✳ ✳ ✳ ✳ ✳ ✳ ✳ ✳

Mary Lombardo is a retired teacher who has taught all grades from 1 through 6 and has taught reading to at-risk students. For several years she worked in an alternative public school program for homeschooled students, providing curriculum and teaching assistance to parents and half-day instruction to students. She also served as a teacher trainer for the Albuquerque Public Schools.

Mary is proof that life after retirement is busier than ever. She writes, works as a volunteer mediator, presents plays to seniors with a reader's theater group, records seniors' histories for their families, volunteers in church and civic groups, and travels with her husband, Nick, whenever they can. Mary has three adult children, who all live in the Southwest.

How to Use this Book

Be a magician!

Before telling your students they are going to learn how to do magic tricks, perform some of the tricks in Chapters I through V and impress your class with your magical powers. The tricks are easy to do; most of the props are already in your classroom or home, and easy-to-follow directions for the tricks are written step by step.

Present the student introduction.

Use the teacher script as a student introduction to stimulate class interest in learning to do the magic tricks.

Review the basic math operations that are listed here.

Many of the magic tricks are based on the fundamental operations that follow. This would be a good time to practice these operations, as being familiar with them will make the reasoning behind the tricks easier to understand.

1. Doubling a number and then dividing it in half brings back the original number. To double a number, multiply it by 2. To halve a number, divide it by 2.

Example:
$6 \times 2 = 12$ (doubling)
and
$12 \div 2 = 6$ (halving)

2. Adding a group of *evenly spaced* numbers and then dividing the sum by how many numbers you added gives the center number.

Example:
$7 + 11 + 15 = 33$
There are 3 evenly spaced numbers.
$33 \div 3 = 11$
11 is the center number.

3. With three *evenly spaced* numbers, subtracting the amount between the numbers from the third number and adding it to the first number gives three numbers equal to the center one.

Example:

7, 11, 15 are spaced 4 numbers apart.

15 - 4 = 11 and 7 + 4 = 11

4. Multiplying a number by 10 always gives that number plus a zero.

Example:

$3 \times 10 = \underline{30}$

$5 \times 10 = \underline{50}$

Once you've reviewed and practiced the preceding operations, it's time to get into the magic!

Start with the easiest tricks in Chapter I.

The first few tricks in Chapter I, One-Timers, are the simplest. They are a good introduction to the magic unit. Perform the first one, Flip 'Em Over, a few times and ask the students how they think the magic works. Test any ideas to see if they are correct.

Go over the directions step by step, either reading them to the students or copying the directions for use on an overhead projector and reading them together. The students should practice the trick in pairs or small groups. If no correct theories have been advanced, again ask if anyone can guess what makes the trick work.

After reading the explanation of how the trick works under the heading "Why does this work?" see if the students can write an equation to express the math behind the magic. Copy and distribute the student handout. Complete the "How did you do?" section together, with students writing the answers on their copies of the handout in their own words. Continue in this manner with the remainder of the tricks in the first five chapters.

Use Chapter VII as an additional resource.

At any time during the magic unit, refer to Chapter VII for math games that give the opportunity to practice math skills. After the students have learned many of the magic tricks, you may want to encourage interest in pursuing math careers by inviting members of the community to speak to the class about how they use math in their work. Perhaps the students can entertain the speakers with a few of their magic tricks!

Teacher Introduction

* * * * * * * * * * *

The successful completion of most magic tricks depends a great deal on diversion. A skilled magician will divert the audience's attention so tricks can be performed without anyone seeing or deducing exactly what is happening. *Mastering Math through Magic* uses diversion, too. Each trick in this book uses some form of diversion so that even though the tricks are simple, the audience cannot guess how the magic is performed.

As students focus on learning magic tricks, they don't realize that they are improving their knowledge of how numbers work and practicing basic math skills. Learning by doing something enjoyable is an effective way to learn and retain information and skills. This book provides a fun way to review and practice math skills for everyday use, as well as for the math and reading testing that is federally mandated in grades 3 through 8.

You can use this book in several ways:

- Use the tricks to practice math skills in the classroom with every student checking to see that the math done by the magician and volunteer is correct.
- Present a simple or an extravagant magic show.
- Plan an entire integrated unit around the magic tricks.
- Give individual students the directions for a trick and the time to perform it in class as a fun reward for some job well done.

The National Council of Teachers of Mathematics (NCTM) suggests that to keep students interested in math, present them with activities that will interest and challenge them as well as help them develop a sense of numbers. Whichever way you decide to use the information in this book, you will be following that suggestion.

Organization of the Book

In the "If You Decide to Present a Magic Show" section of this book, you will find a "Teacher Script for Student Information." This provides general information on how to get started as a magician, the language to use, what to wear, and how to perform the tricks.

Five chapters of tricks follow. Each chapter begins with notes to the teacher presenting the math skills that will be practiced in the chapter. The notes also rate the complexity of the tricks so they can be assigned to ensure that all students find challenge and success. A "Teacher Script" for introducing each chapter to the students follows the "Teacher Notes."

Chapter I includes tricks that are very simple. If you are presenting a magic show, these tricks should be done one time only, as the answer is always the same. The tricks in Chapter II use calendars. Those in Chapter III involve the use of dice. Coins are the basis of the magic in Chapter IV. Chapter V is an assortment of tricks that don't fit in any of the prior categories.

The tricks are written in easy-to-follow, step-by-step instructions. Each trick begins with a short introductory statement for the students to announce what they plan to do. The tricks are organized in a three-part format:

1. **THE PROPS** tells what materials are needed to do the trick.
2. **THE TRICK** gives step-by-step directions for performing the trick with suggestions for what the students should say.
3. **THE MAGIC** explains how the trick works mathematically.

Examples and illustrations are included to help the teacher explain how the tricks work and to make performing and understanding the tricks easier. At the end of each trick, a student handout contains questions under the heading "How did you do?" which the students should answer in their own words. This exercise gives them the opportunity to review what they have done and to demonstrate that they understand the math reasoning behind the trick by writing the math equations they used.

Chapter VI divulges mysteries about the number 9 and two easy ways to learn the 9 times table. Students also will learn a method for using the 6 through 9 times tables without having to memorize them.

Chapter VII contains games that you will find useful for those times when you have a few minutes before beginning another activity or before dismissal. In addition, there are games written in easy-to-follow directions for your students to play in groups of two or more. All the games are related to math functions.

The book ends with a listing of tricks indexed according to the math skill practiced.

Objectives

This book was written with the following objectives in mind:

1. Correlate teaching and learning activities with the concepts contained in the math standards as set forth by the National Council of Teachers of Mathematics.

The National Council of Teachers of Mathematics (NCTM) has developed a set of 10 standards for math learning from pre-kindergarten through grade 12. The tricks in *Mastering Math through Magic* correlate with the concepts presented in these standards.

2. Teach children that working with numbers can be fun.

When students look forward to presenting magic tricks, they approach the task with pleasure, not fear, and build confidence in their ability to work with numbers.

3. Cultivate a sense of numbers.

Number sense is a familiarity with how numbers work. Students with number sense can predict what will happen in number situations and have increased flexibility when working with numbers.

4. Increase fluency in mental manipulation of numbers.

As students become more familiar with the logical way that numbers work, they will be able to do many math functions mentally.

5. Understand the relationships between number operations.

Many of the tricks depend on reversing operations to make the "magic" work. Students see that addition and subtraction, multiplication and division, and doubling and halving are opposites.

6. Provide an opportunity for students to write about what they have done and learned.

Research shows that writing about math operations cements understanding. After each trick, students write about their performance and review the mathematical reasons and equations that make the trick work.

7. Improve confidence in one's knowledge of numbers by successfully participating in performance of magic tricks.

Subject matter is best learned and remembered through play. Because students are focused on mastering a magic trick, they are more relaxed about learning. Complexity of the tricks varies so all children are challenged and can participate successfully.

Correlation with National Math Standards

The tricks, games, and the suggested processes for creating mathematical games and designing magic tricks in *Mastering Math through Magic* correspond to the concepts presented in the math standards issued by the NCTM for students from pre-kindergarten through grade 12. In the listings that follow, the corresponding math concepts are shown in bold print.

For a complete description of the math standards, refer to the NCTM Web site at <www.nctm.org>.

Correlation of Magic Tricks to Math Concepts

In the following listing, all of the tricks in this book correlate with every concept with the exception of Magic Toothpicks and Magic Fingers. These two tricks are based on trickery, not math functions. They are included to provide a bit of humor!

NUMBER AND OPERATIONS

The math that underlies the magic in each trick demonstrates how numbers and number relationships work. Because each trick involves performing math operations, the tricks also encourage facility and accuracy in computing.

PROBLEM SOLVING

After each trick is performed and before the math explanation is read, students are asked to formulate a mathematical theory of why the magic works. As they theorize about the math operations used in the tricks, they use problem-solving techniques, and build and review mathematical knowledge.

REASONING AND PROOF

The students conjecture about how the tricks work mathematically and evaluate their guesses to determine if they can prove they are correct.

COMMUNICATION

After each trick, the students complete a handout explaining in their own words the math that makes the magic work. Their communication must be clear, and they must demonstrate that they understand the math reasoning.

CONNECTIONS

All of the tricks use interconnecting mathematical ideas and operations. The connections between division and multiplication, subtraction and addition, doubling and halving are clearly shown.

REPRESENTATION

The math operations in all of the tricks can be represented pictorially or by using objects. Representation is strongly suggested for the following tricks to help students understand the math processes. These tricks are:

- Hidden Coins

- Leftovers, Anyone?

- Heads or Tails

- Share Magic

Correlation of Games and Creating New Games and Tricks to Math Concepts

As students use their creativity and math knowledge to play and create new games, and to invent magic tricks, they

1. demonstrate that they understand number operations (**NUMBER AND OPERATIONS**);

2. use a variety of strategies to win games as well as to create viable games and tricks (**PROBLEM SOLVING**);

3. show or prove why their mathematical conjectures work (**REASONING AND PROOF**);

4. communicate their math ideas through explaining how a game is played or by performing a magic trick (**COMMUNICATION**); and

5. use connections between number ideas and operations to design games and tricks, as well as representation and measurement skills to design games (**CONNECTIONS, REPRESENTA-TION, MEASUREMENT**).

If You Decide to Present a Magic Show

✶ ✶ ✶ ✶ ✶ ✶ ✶ ✶ ✶ ✶ ✶

Putting on a magic show does not have to be a big production. You have many options:

OPTION 1. The easiest way to have a magic show is to assign one trick to each student and present the tricks within your own classroom. Choose days when performances will be held and post a sign-up sheet so students can select when they want to perform. The advantages for doing it this way are:

- children have a chance to perform in front of an audience without using much class time;
- all students practice math skills as they check to see that the magician and the volunteer are doing the math operations correctly; and
- the magicians can explain the math process to their classmates, providing another opportunity to review skills and thought processes.

OPTION 2. Another fairly easy way to put on a show is to divide your class into several groups with each group responsible for a different chapter in the book. These groups can present their tricks to various classes in the school with each child responsible for assembling and carrying his or her own props.

One of the magicians also can act as emcee to start off the show. That child introduces the show and the first performer. Each child in turn, after performing his or her own magic trick, introduces the next person who will perform. The last person to perform is the emcee who closes the show, thanking the audience for its attention.

OPTION 3. The most time-consuming way to have a show is for each student in your class to learn one or more tricks and as a whole perform for other individual classes or at a school assembly. While this does take more planning and time, presenting a show of this nature will be one of your students' favorite memories of school.

If your class has organized and presented a show at your school, you might want to share the magic with others. Senior citizen centers or retirement homes are good venues for this type of show as are libraries that often offer presentations for school field trips.

Whichever option you choose, you won't have to worry that the assignment is a waste of study time. Learning how to perform the tricks can be done during the school day or can be assigned for homework or a combination of both. The tricks that your students will learn and practice fulfill every requirement for valuable study by furthering their understanding of how numbers work and raising their comfort level for math. In addition, motivation will be high and attitude will be positive, two of the most important factors for effective learning.

The Props

Most of the tricks call only for paper and marker. Using a large piece of paper posted where the audience can see it and using a dark colored marker are good ideas for two reasons. One, the audience can check to make sure the volunteer is following the directions and doing the math right—two points vital to the successful completion of the trick. Two, the audience will be able to see right away that the young magicians have done exactly what they said they would do.

Other simple props are pages from a calendar, preferably a large wall calendar so that the pages can be posted for the audience to see; a clock or picture of a clock face; coins, stones, or dried beans; regular dice; and toothpicks.

With tricks that use small objects such as coins or beans, use an overhead projector so the audience can see what is going on in the trick. If this is not possible, make sure the magician keeps the audience informed about what is happening.

In Chapter III. Calendar Capers, you will need to cut out a box that can be laid over a calendar page to show nine horizontal numbers on the calendar. This is the only prop that has to be made. All others are easily found at home or in the classroom.

The Dress

No matter what kind of show you plan, your young magicians will be concerned about what to wear. Ask the children to recall magicians they have seen perform on television or in person, and to describe what they wore. You might even take them to the library to find books about magicians to see the many different kinds of magician apparel. Some magicians are casual, wearing everyday clothes. Some magicians wear robes and turbans, some wear tails and a top hat, and others wear a nice suit or dress.

The important thing to stress to your students is that whatever they choose to wear must be comfortable. If they have to worry about how their clothes are fitting or if the clothes have to be constantly adjusted, they won't be able to concentrate on performing the tricks. To keep the costuming simple, students can wear their everyday school clothes or dress clothes. Pairing black pants and a black shirt makes another good magician outfit.

Making Costumes

If your students want to wear costumes, here are some ideas for making a star-studded cape, a bow tie, a top hat, and a turban. You will need the following materials:

- black oak-tag
- black construction and crepe papers
- black ribbon or string
- aluminum foil
- star stickers

To make a cape:

1. Measure enough black crepe paper to cover the back of the student twice from shoulder to shoulder.
2. Lay a long piece of string or ribbon along the top edge, fold over about two inches, and either tape or staple a hem, making sure not to catch the ribbon in the staples so it can be used to gather the cape.
3. Decorate the cape with star stickers, and larger star and moon cutouts from the aluminum foil. Attach the moons and stars with pieces of masking tape rolled so that both sides are sticky.
4. Gather the paper by pulling the ribbon from each side so the cape now covers the student's back and shoulders, and tie the ribbon in front.

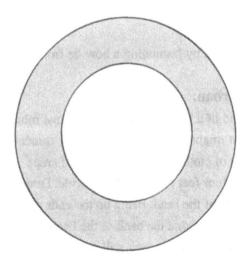

To make a top hat:

1. Using a large piece of black oak-tag, cut out a wide circle, the center of which fits on the student's head. This will be the hat's brim.

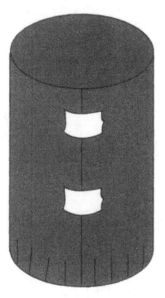

2. Take a large piece of construction paper and tape it into a cylinder so that it fits in the circle you have cut. This is the top of the hat. Cut it down a few inches if it is too tall. Cut one-inch wide slits all around one end.

3. When you fold up the cut pieces and glue them onto the bottom of the brim, the top hat is ready to wear. Additional stars and ky shapes can be pasted to the underside of the brim.

4. Complete the hat by fashioning a bow tie from crepe paper of any color. Voila! Instant magician!

To make a turban:

A turban instead of a top hat makes the costume more exotic, and that might appeal to some of your students.

1. Take a piece of cloth, a scarf, or a piece of crepe paper about four feet long and a foot wide. Drape it over the front of the head. Bring up the ends and crisscross them around the back of the head, then around the front as far as they will go. Tuck the ends under. A star sticker or aluminum foil cutout can be taped to the front of the turban.

Patter

A magic show is not just about doing magic tricks. The audience must be warmed up and put in a receptive frame of mind. One of the best ways to do this is for the performers to tell jokes or relate amusing incidents that have happened to them.

You can use one of your library periods to find joke books suitable for your young magicians to use, or you can assign this task as homework. Ask the students to choose several jokes, memorize them, and practice telling them.

Another homework assignment is for students to write one or more essays telling about something funny that has happened to them. If they intend to use some of these stories in their performance, they should practice telling them aloud.

The students also will have to create their own magic words to use as they perform their tricks. This would be a good time for a lesson in alliteration and rhyming. See The Language of Magic section in "Teacher Script for Student Introduction" for suggestions.

When they are learning the tricks, the students also should practice how they will give the directions for doing the tricks. Each trick includes suggested statements that the students can read, or they can make up their own patter as they work through the tricks.

Practice is very important. You cannot emphasize this point enough. The students should practice the jokes. They should practice what they will say throughout the trick. They should practice performing the trick. If they will be wearing a costume, they should have at least one practice session wearing it.

Using *Mastering Math through Magic* can be a valuable part of your math instruction. There is no better way to make students comfortable with working with numbers than to have them practice math skills in an enjoyable format, such as preparing for a magic show. You can enjoy the fun of a magic performance knowing that your students are learning.

Teacher Script for Student Introduction

You are going to become magicians. You will learn some mind-boggling magic tricks that will amaze your friends. Your friends will be asking, "How did you do that?" Of course, you won't tell because the secret to being a good magician is never revealing how the tricks work.

The tricks that you're going to learn will be easy for you to do, but it will be hard for your friends to figure out how you work your magic. You will be able to add numbers that you can't see, guess a secret number that someone has chosen, tell which numbers are rolled on dice without looking at the dice, and many more mystical tricks.

Some of the tricks you will do are simple and some are more challenging, but I promise you they are all puzzling and astonishing!

Getting Started

If you've watched some of the great magicians perform, you know that they don't just stand up and perform a magic trick. They usually tell the audience what to expect before they do the trick and might tell a few jokes or stories to get everyone laughing and in a good mood.

Successful magicians rehearse and rehearse before they perform. They don't just practice their tricks. They also practice what they will say to the audience. You will want to do the same thing. You can find some good joke books at the library. Choose some jokes you like and memorize them. Practice telling the jokes and talking about what you will do in the trick. Do the tricks several times before you perform them for an audience, and your show will go smoother than a speedy slide across slippery ice.

Another thing to remember is not to reveal the answer to the trick too soon. Scratch your head, rub your chin and frown, as if you are thinking very hard before saying some magic words and revealing the answer. Acting this way will make the tricks seem more mystifying to your audience.

The Language of Magic

How do you learn the magic words to say? You make them up! Honest!

Magicians often use words that sound magical just before they demonstrate their magic powers. "Abracadabra, hocus pocus" are some famous magic words that you've probably heard many times. Just like famous magicians, you can make up and use any magic words you like. Try some rhymes like

"Beetle juice and bat's wings,
I am the master of magical things."

Or just string some words together that start with the same letter and sound good like

"Suffering saliva and salamander soup."

What Do Magicians Wear?

Now, what about clothes? What should you wear when you perform? Some magicians wear capes and top hats. Some dress in everyday clothes.

You can dress in a special outfit, something that you usually don't wear to school. Or, you can borrow or make clothes that you think are just the thing for a magician to wear. If you decide you want to make a special outfit, I can help you with some ideas.

Whatever outfit you decide on, make sure you are comfortable in it, and don't worry about looking like a magician. Your tricks will show you are a real magician no matter what you are wearing.

Learning the Magic Tricks

I have a book that gives clear directions for doing many magic tricks. Each trick begins with one sentence that you can use to announce what you will be doing in the trick. The directions for the tricks include some suggestions for what to say to your audience before and during the trick. Many of the directions for doing the tricks are short and easy, so you will be able to memorize the steps. Some of the tricks have more involved directions, so you might want to copy the steps onto small index cards that you can read from as you perform the trick.

We will need some props or materials to do each trick. Everything we need is either somewhere in our classroom, or your house, or they are things that you can make or get easily.

For each trick in the book, there is a section called The Magic. This explains, *for our eyes only,* how the trick works and gives you a place to write about how you performed the trick.

Now, on to the magic!

Chapter I
ONE-TIMERS

✳ ✳ ✳ ✳ ✳ ✳ ✳ ✳ ✳ ✳

Teacher Notes

There are 10 tricks in this chapter. All but a few use single step math processes. All the tricks are easy to perform and understand.

Trick 1. Flip 'Em Over: Simple Subtraction

Without looking, the magician will say what the sum of five numbers is after one has been changed.

Trick 2. Flip 'Em Backward: Simple Addition

This is the same as Trick 1 done with different numbers.

Trick 3. Clock Opposites: Simple Subtraction, Division, and Multiplication

The magician correctly tells the answer after a volunteer finds the difference between two numbers on a clock and changes it through division and multiplication.

Trick 4. Magic Toothpicks: A Play on Words

This is really not a magic trick at all, but a play on words, which is fun for the performer and the audience. It is very easy to do.

Trick 5. Where Do You Live? Addition, Subtraction, Multiplication, and Division

The magician will be able to tell what the answer is after a volunteer has changed the numbers from his or her address by adding, subtracting, multiplying, and dividing them.

Trick 6. Triple Trouble: Subtraction with Borrowing

A secret number is changed through reversing it and addition and subtraction, but the magician will be able to tell what the final answer is.

Trick 7. How Old Are You? Subtraction with Borrowing

The magician predicts the answer to a math problem that begins with a person's age.

Trick 8. Tricky Two-Step: Subtraction with Borrowing and Addition with Carrying

The magician predicts the final answer to a math problem after the original number has been changed through subtraction and addition.

Trick 9. Summing It Up: Addition with Carrying

The magician will be able to tell the final answer to a math problem that is all about dates.

Trick 10. Words and Numbers: Simple Addition and Spelling

The magician will predict the final number of a trick that takes several steps.

None of the tricks in this chapter should be performed more than once during a performance because the answers to their puzzles are always the same. They serve as an easy introduction to the remainder of the tricks in *Mastering Math through Magic*.

✳ ✳ ✳ ✳ ✳ ✳ ✳ ✳ ✳ ✳

Teacher Script

The first 10 magic tricks you will learn are tricks that you should perform only once each time you do your magic tricks. They are very simple tricks, great for warming up an audience, but the answer to each trick is always the same. If you perform them more than once, the audience will probably guess how the magic works, and you want to keep that your secret.

Remember that each trick is followed by an explanation of what makes it work. After we learn each trick but before we read that explanation, we'll take a few minutes to try to figure out the secret ourselves. It'll be fun to see if we can do that.

But don't worry. Even if you can figure it out, your audience will not be able to. That's because, when you perform magic tricks in a show, you don't give the audience time to think about anything. You perform one trick after another with very little time between tricks. Your magic secrets will be safe.

Now we're ready to begin to perform magic.

Flip 'Em Over: Simple Subtraction

Say: **In this trick I will show that I don't have to look at numbers to add them and get the right answer.**

THE PROPS

- You will need five strips of paper about six inches long and one inch wide.
- On the first piece of paper, write 1 on one side. Turn it over and write 2 on the other side.
- On the next piece of paper, write 3 on one side and 4 on the other side.
- On the next piece of paper, write 5 on one side and 6 on the other side.
- Do the same for the numbers 7 and 8, and 9 and 10.

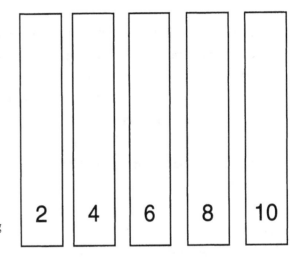

Figure 1.1 Strips of Paper with Even Numbers Showing

THE TRICK

1. Tape the papers to a wall or chart so the audience can see them with only the even numbers (2, 4, 6, 8, 10) showing. The numbers showing add up to 30.
2. Give a volunteer a small piece of tape and put on a blindfold or turn your back so you cannot see the papers.
3. Say to the volunteer: **Please turn over one piece of paper and tape it again to the wall. Add the numbers you see on all the slips of paper. Let me know when you're ready, but don't tell me the answer.**
4. When the volunteer is ready, say: **Even though I can't see which piece of paper you have turned over, I can tell you the sum of all the numbers.**
5. Say some magic words and pretend you are thinking very hard. Then announce that the sum of your numbers is 29.

THE MAGIC

The answer in this trick will always be 29.

Why does this work?

The numbers showing on the papers total 30. The number on the backside of each slip of paper is 1 less than the number on top. So, no matter which strip of paper is turned over, the answer will always be one less than 30. It's simple subtraction. One less than 30 is, of course, 29 ($30 - 1 = 29$).

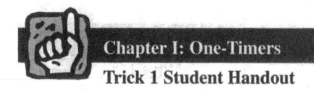
Flip 'Em Over: Simple Subtraction

Name _____ Date _____

Now you try it:

1. Fix five strips of paper so that even numbers are written on one side and odd numbers on the reverse side. The numerals 1 and 2 are on the same paper, 3 and 4 on another, 5 and 6 on another, 7 and 8 on another, and 9 and 10 on the last.
2. Lay out the five pieces of paper with the even numbers 2, 4, 6, 8 and 10 showing.
3. Add the numbers. You should reach the sum of 30.
4. Turn over one piece of paper to show the odd number written on the other side.
5. Is the sum of the numbers now 29? It has to be because numbers always work in a logical manner, and 1 less than 30 is 29.

How did you do?

Materials (What props did you use?)

Procedure (How did you do the trick?)

Conclusion (What makes the trick work?)

Equations (What equations did you use to make the trick work?)

Flip 'Em Backward: Simple Addition

Say: **Just to show I really can add numbers without looking at them, I'm going to do it again**.

THE PROPS

Use the same numbered slips of paper you used in the first trick. But this time use the reverse side so the odd numbers show. Remember, 1 and 2 are on the same paper, 3 and 4 on another, 5 and 6 on another, 7 and 8 on another, and 9 and 10 on the last.

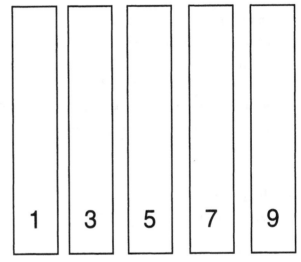

Figure 1.2 Strips of Paper with Odd Numbers Showing

THE TRICK

1. Tape the slips of paper to the wall or chart just the way you did for the last trick, only this time let the odd numbers show (1, 3, 5, 7, 9). The sum of the numbers should be 25.
2. Give the volunteer a small piece of tape and turn your back or put on your blindfold.
3. Say: **Turn over one piece of paper and tape it again to the wall. Add the numbers you see. Tell me when you are ready, but do not tell me the answer.**
4. When the volunteer tells you he is ready, say: **Even though I cannot see what you have done, I will tell you the sum of the numbers.**
5. Say some magic words. Then announce that the answer is 26.

THE MAGIC

The answer to this trick will always be 26.

Why does this work?

The sum of the odd numbers is 25. The bottom numbers on each paper are 1 more than the numbers that are on top. No matter which paper is turned over, 1 more will be added. The answer will always be 1 more than 25, which is 26 (1 + 25 = 26).

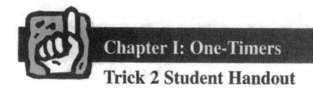
Flip 'Em Backward: Simple Addition

Name _____ Date _____

Now you try it:

1. Fix five pieces of paper so that even numbers are written on one side and odd numbers on the reverse side. The numerals 1 and 2 are on the same paper, 3 and 4 on another, 5 and 6 on another, 7 and 8 on another, and 9 and 10 on the last.

2. Lay out the five pieces of paper with the odd numbers 1, 3, 5, 7, and 9 showing.

3. Turn over one piece of paper so the even number written on the other side shows.

4. Is the sum of the numbers now 26? Of course it is. Remember, numbers work in a logical way.

How did you do?

Materials (What props did you use?)

Procedure (How did you do the trick?)

Conclusion (What makes the trick work?)

Equations (What equations did you use to make the trick work?)

Clock Opposites: Simple Subtraction, Division, and Multiplication

Say: **I will get the right answer to the work you do with numbers even though you will not tell me what number you start with.**

THE PROPS

dark-colored marker

clock or a drawing of a clock

large piece of paper posted where the audience can see it (If you don't have a large piece of paper, tape two or more regular-sized sheets together.)

THE TRICK

1. Ask for a volunteer and show that person the clock, then turn your back.
2. Say: **Please choose two opposite numbers on the clock and write them on the paper.**
3. Say: **Subtract the smaller number from the larger. Then add 14.**
4. Say: **Divide that number by 2.**
5. Say: **Now multiply your answer by 3.**
6. Say: **Now subtract 5 from your answer and tell me when you are ready.**
7. When the person has the answer, say some magic words. Then announce that the answer is 25.

Figure 1.3 Opposite Numbers on a Clock Face

THE MAGIC

Because you know that the difference between opposite numbers on a clock is always 6, it's easy to get the answer to this trick.

Why does this work?

There are 12 hours on the clock. Opposite numbers are half of the clock away from each other so they are half of 12, which is 6. You know the number the person starts with. Then the volunteer adds and subtracts numbers you give, so you are always in control of what the answer will be. The answer is always 25 in this trick if you use the numbers given. If you decide to change the numbers, figure out what the new answer will be before you do the trick.

Example:

The volunteer starts with the number 6.

Then 14 is added.	$6 + 14 = 20$
The answer is divided by 2.	$20 \div 2 = 10$
That answer is multiplied by 3.	$3 \times 10 = 30$
The last step is to subtract 5.	$30 - 5 = 25$

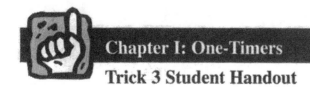
Clock Opposites: Simple Subtraction, Division, and Multiplication

Name _____ Date _____

Look at all the opposite numbers on the clock. 12 is opposite 6; 1 is opposite 7; 2 is opposite 8; 3 is opposite 9; 4 is opposite 10; 5 is opposite 11; and 6 is opposite 12. Is the difference between each pair of numbers always a 6? Yes, it is, because the numbers are halfway around the clock from each other, which is half of 12, or 6.

Now you try it:

1. Choose two numbers on the clock.
2. Subtract the smaller one from the larger one.
3. Add 14.
4. Divide your answer by 2.
5. Multiply your answer by 3.
6. Subtract 5.
7. Is the answer 25?

How did you do?

Materials (What props did you use?)

Procedure (How did you do the trick?)

Conclusion (What makes the trick work?)

Equations (What equations did you use to make the trick work?)

Magic Toothpicks: A Play on Words

This is a trick that isn't magical, but it's fun to do anyway, just for laughs.

Say: **I can change nine toothpicks into ten!**

THE PROPS

nine toothpicks

an overhead projector if you are performing the trick for a large audience

THE TRICK

1. Lay nine toothpicks in a row on a table or on an overhead projector.

2. Say to your audience: **Here are nine toothpicks. Can anyone here turn nine toothpicks into ten?**

3. When no one in your audience can do it, say some magic words while you show them how it's done. (See the picture.)

THE MAGIC

You make the audience think you will make ten toothpicks out of nine, but you will make ten a different way!

Why does this work?

You move the toothpicks around so they spell the word *ten*. The picture shows you how.

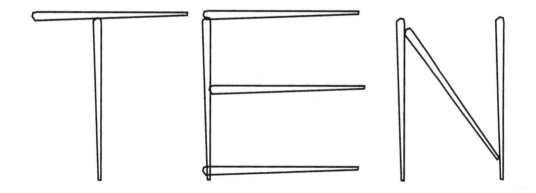

Figure 1.4 Arrangement of Toothpicks

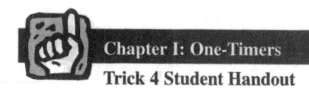

Magic Toothpicks: A Play on Words

Name _____ Date _____

Now you try it:

1. Place nine toothpicks on a table.

2. Arrange the nine toothpicks to spell the word *ten* just as it shows in the picture.

How did you do?

Materials (What props did you use?)

Procedure (How did you do the trick?)

Conclusion (What makes the trick work?)

Where Do You Live? Addition, Subtraction, Multiplication, and Division

Say: **You are going to start with the numbers in your address and change them by adding, multiplying, subtracting, and dividing them. No matter what you do, I will be able to tell what your final answer is.**

THE PROPS

dark-colored marker

large piece of paper hung so the audience can see it

THE TRICK

1. Put the paper where the audience can see what is being written on it. Turn your back and ask a volunteer to write the numbers from her address on the paper.
2. Say: **Add the number 7 to your address.**
3. Say: **Multiply the answer by 2.**
4. Say: **Now subtract 2.**
5. Say: **Divide your answer by 2.**
6. Say: **The last thing you will do is subtract your address from the last answer.**
7. After you say your magic words, announce that the final answer is 6.

THE MAGIC

This trick has nothing at all to do with the street number. The street number is just used so that the audience will not guess what you are doing with the other numbers.

Why does this work?

If you leave out the street number and multiply 7 by 2, then subtract 2 and divide by 2, the answer is 6.

Example:

$$7 \times 2 = 14$$
$$14 - 2 = 12$$
$$12 \div 2 = 6$$

Since you start with the street number and then subtract it, it does not change your answer, which will always be 6. The street numbers are put in just to trick the audience.

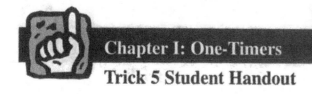
Where Do You Live? Addition, Subtraction, Multiplication, and Division

Name _____ Date _____

Now you try it:

1. Write down your street number.
2. Add 7 to that number.
3. Multiply your answer by 2.
4. Subtract 2.
5. Divide the answer by 2.
6. Subtract your street address.
7. Your answer is 6, isn't it? Congratulations! You are a very good magician.

How did you do?

Materials (What props did you use?)

Procedure (How did you do the trick?)

Conclusion (What makes the trick work?)

Equations (What equations did you use to make the trick work?)

Triple Trouble: Subtraction with Borrowing

Say: You are going to choose any number you want and change it by turning it around and adding and subtracting it, but you won't fool me. I will be able to tell you what your final answer is.

PROPS

dark-colored marker, large piece of paper

THE TRICK

1. Put the paper where the audience can see what is being written on it.
2. Give the volunteer a marker and put on your blindfold.
3. Say: **Write three different numbers between 1 and 9 so that you have a three-digit number with the largest number first and the smallest number last.**

Example: 742

4. Say: **Reverse that three-digit number so that the smallest number is now first and the largest one is now last. Write that under the first number and subtract it from the top number.**

Example: 742 − 247 = 495

3. Say: **Now add the three digits in your answer.**

Example: 4 + 9 + 5

4. Without taking off your blindfold, say some magic words. Then announce that the answer is 18.

THE MAGIC

When a three-digit number is reversed and the smaller one subtracted from the larger one, the sum of the digits in the answer is always 18.

Why does this work?

When you reverse the numbers, the middle digit stays the same: 7<u>4</u>2 and 2<u>4</u>7

But the final digit of the top number is smaller than the final digit of the bottom number.

$$742$$
$$- 247$$

So when you subtract, you will need to borrow. Because the middle number is the same on the top and the bottom, borrowing makes the middle digit in your answer come out as a 9.

$$742$$
$$- 247$$
$$495$$

(Nines can be very mysterious. See chapter VI if you don't believe me!)

The borrowing makes the other numbers in your answer total 9, too:

$$4 + 5 = 9$$

Since 9 plus 9 equals 18, you will always have the right answer handy.

Triple Trouble: Subtraction with Borrowing

Name _____ Date _____

Now you try it:

1. Write a three-digit number with the largest digit first and the smallest last.

Example: 321

2. Reverse the number and subtract the smaller one from the larger one.

Example: 321 − 123

3. Do the digits in your answer add up to 18? Of course they do. You are never wrong when you do math magic!

How did you do?

Materials (What props did you use?)

Procedure (How did you do the trick?)

Conclusion (What makes the magic work?)

Equations (What equations did you use to make the trick work?)

How Old Are You?
Subtraction with Borrowing

Say: **I will be able to predict the answer to a math problem even though we will start with your age, and I don't know how old you are.**

THE PROPS

dark-colored marker

small piece of paper

large piece of paper posted where the audience can see it

THE TRICK

1. Write the number 9 on a small piece of paper. Fold the paper and ask someone in the audience to hold it until you ask him to open it.
2. Say: **This is my prediction for the answer to this number problem.**
3. Ask for a volunteer who is older than 13. Tell the person not to tell you his age.
4. Say: **Write down your age, then reverse the digits and subtract the smaller number from the larger one.**
5. Say: **Add the two digits in the answer.**
6. Now ask the person in the audience to whom you gave the paper to unfold it and read your prediction out loud. Of course your prediction was correct! After all, you are a magician!

THE MAGIC

This is another trick that works because you have to borrow when you subtract.

Why does this work?

When you reverse a number and subtract the smaller one from the bigger one, you will always have to borrow. When you subtract reversed numbers you will always get 9 or digits that add up to 9.

Example: $41 - 14 = 27$ and $2 + 7 = 9$

Note: This trick will not work if the person's age contains two numbers that are the same (22, 33, 55, etc.).

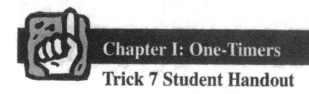
How Old Are You?
Subtraction with Borrowing

Name _____ Date _____

Now you try it:

1. Write down any age that is over 13 that does not contain the same two digits such as 22 or 55. Use the example as a guide, but try it yourself with a different number.

Example: 25

2. Reverse it and subtract the smaller from the larger number.

Example: 52 − 25 = 27

3. Add the two digits in the answer.

Example: 2 + 7 = 9

4. Your answer is 9, right? Of course it is. You are never wrong!

How did you do?

Materials (What props did you use?)

Procedure (How did you do the trick?)

Conclusion (What makes the magic work?)

Equations (What equations did you use to make the trick work?)

Tricky Two-Step: Subtraction with Borrowing and Addition with Carrying

Say: **I will predict the answer to the math problem you will do even though I do not know what numbers you will choose.**

THE PROPS

dark-colored marker

a small piece of paper

a large piece of paper hung where the audience can see it

THE TRICK

1. Write the number 1089 on a piece of paper and fold it. Don't reveal the number. Make a big show of folding the paper and giving it to a member of the audience to hold.

2. Say: **The number I have written on this paper is my prediction for the answer to the number problem we are going to do.**

3. Ask for a volunteer and give her a marker.

4. Say: **Write down a three-digit number using three different digits. None of them can be a zero.**

5. Say: **Reverse the number and subtract the smaller one from the larger one.**

6. Say: **Now reverse the answer and add those two numbers.**

Example:

462 reverses to 264

462 − 264 = 198

198 reverses to 891

198 + 891 = 1089

7. Ask the person in the audience to open the paper and read out loud the prediction you wrote. Of course, you are correct! Take a deep bow. You deserve it!

THE MAGIC

This is yet another trick that depends on borrowing to make it come out as you wish.

Why does this work?

Just as we did in the last two tricks, we asked the volunteer to reverse two numbers and subtract them. We know that the digits in the answer will all add up to 9. When the numbers are again reversed and this time added, the numbers in the 1's column will always add up to 9, the two 9s in the center column will always add up to 18, and the final column (because you have to carry the 1) will add up to 10. You end up with 1089.

Tricky Two-Step: Subtraction with Borrowing and Addition with Carrying

Name _____ Date _____

Now you try it:

1. Write a three-digit number with no zeros in it. Use the example as a guide, but try it yourself with a different number.

Example: 447

2. Reverse the number and subtract the smaller number from the larger one.

Example: 744 − 447 = 297

3. Reverse that number and add it to the last answer.

Example: 792 + 297 = 1089

4. Is your answer 1089 just as it is in the example? It should be if you added and subtracted carefully.

How did you do?

Materials (What props did you use?)

Procedure (How did you do the trick?)

Conclusion (What makes the magic work?)

Equations (What equations did you use to make the trick work?)

Summing It Up: Addition with Carrying

Say: **I will predict the correct sum to numbers we haven't picked or added yet.**

THE PROPS

dark-colored marker

large piece of paper posted where the audience can see it

small piece of paper

THE TRICK

1. Double the number of the present year and write it on a piece of paper. Don't reveal the number you wrote. Make a big show of folding the paper and giving it to a member of the audience to hold.

2. Say: **The number I have written on this paper is my prediction for the answer to the number problem we are going to do.**

3. Choose a volunteer and say: **Please write down the year you were born.**

4. Say: **Below that year, in a column, write a year when something important happened to you.**

5. Say: **Please write below that how old you will be on your birthday this year.**

6. Say: **Please write below that the number of years that have passed since the year that something important happened to you.**

7. Ask the volunteer to add the four numbers.

8. Say: **Would the person who is holding my prediction please unfold the paper and read the number out loud.**

9. Your prediction will be the same as the sum of the numbers that have just been added.

THE MAGIC

The answer to this trick will always be double the number of the current year no matter how old or young the volunteer is.

Example:

```
  1990   Born
+ 1995   Learned to ski
+   12   Age this year
+    7   Years since something important happened
  4004
```

Look at the example. If it is the year 2002, the four years the volunteer chose add up to 4004.

Trick 9

Why does this work?

The year when the volunteer was born plus his age this year adds up to the number of the current year. In the example, the volunteer was born in 1990 and is 12 years old in 2002. Those two numbers add up to 2002.

$$\begin{array}{r} 1990 \\ +\ \ 12 \\ \hline 2002 \end{array}$$ the year the volunteer was born
how old the volunteer is this year

The year when the important event happened and the number of years since then also add up to the current year.

$$\begin{array}{r} 1995 \\ +\ \ \ \ 7 \\ \hline 2002 \end{array}$$ when the volunteer learned to ski
years since then

So that is 2 times the current year, which is exactly the prediction you made!

$$2002 \times 2 = 4004 \text{ or } 2002 + 2002 = 4004$$

Summing It Up: Addition with Carrying

Name _____ Date _____

Now you try it:

1. Write down the year you were born.
2. Write down the year something important happened to you.
3. Write down how old you will be this year.
4. For your final number, write down how many years it has been since the year something important happened.
5. Add these four numbers.
6. Is your answer the same as two times the number of the current year? It is if you added and subtracted correctly!

How did you do?

Materials (What props did you use?)

Procedure (How did you do the trick?)

Conclusion (What makes the magic work?)

Equations (What equations did you use to make the trick work?)

Words and Numbers:
Simple Addition and Spelling

Say: **In this trick you will choose a number and change it several times, but I will be able to predict your final number.**

THE PROPS

dark-colored marker

small piece of paper

large piece of paper posted where the audience can see it

THE TRICK

1. Choose a volunteer and say: **You are going to pick a secret number and change it in several ways. But before you do that, I am going to predict your final number.**
2. Take a piece of paper and write the number 4 on it. Don't let anyone see the number you wrote.
3. Fold the paper and give it to someone in the audience to hold. Say: **This is my prediction. Please hold this paper until the trick is over.**
4. Say to the volunteer: **Please choose a number and write it on the paper. You are going to have to spell the number you wrote so make sure you pick a number you can spell.**
5. When the number is written, say: **Now write the word for your number.**
6. Say: **Count the letters in the word you have written and write that number down.**
7. Say: **It's spelling time again. Write the word for your last number.**
8. Say: **Now count the letters in that word and write that number.**
9. Repeat these two steps until the volunteer writes the number 4, the number you predicted.
10. Say: **Would the person who is holding my prediction please stand and read what number I predicted?**
11. When the number 4 is read, take your bow.

THE MAGIC

The answer in this trick will always be 4.

Why does this work?

The word *four* is the only word that has exactly the same number of letters as the number it represents. No matter which number is chosen as the first number in this series, 4 is the only possible last number.

Example:

35

thirty-five

10

ten

3

three

5

five

4

Words and Numbers:
Simple Addition and Spelling

Name _____ Date _____

Now you try it:

1. Pick a number, any number, but make sure you can spell it!

2. Write the number.

3. Write the word for that number.

4. Count how many letters are in the word and write that number.

5. Keep going until you reach the number 4.

How did you do?

Materials (What props did you use?)

Procedure (How did you do the trick?)

Conclusion (What makes the trick work?)

Chapter II
CALENDAR CAPERS

✳ ✳ ✳ ✳ ✳ ✳ ✳ ✳ ✳ ✳

Teacher Notes

The tricks in this chapter are more challenging than those in the first chapter, but not because the math work is harder. The math is just addition and multiplication and division. What makes the tricks more of a challenge is the reasoning behind the "magic," which is an introduction to averaging. All of the tricks use a calendar and work because the numbers on a calendar are in numerical order and evenly spaced, seven numbers apart vertically and one number apart horizontally.

Trick 1. Calendar Opposites: Addition and Doubling
The magician will be able to tell the sum of numbers opposite each other in a 9-number calendar box when told the first number in the box.

Trick 2. Ups and Downs: Multiplication with a One-Digit and Two-Digit Number, Simple Addition and Subtraction
The magician will be able to tell the sum of three columns of three numbers each, after being told only one number.

Trick 3. Dates, Dates, Everywhere: Simple Division, Addition, and Subtraction
After being told the sum of three numbers that someone has chosen on the calendar, the magician will know which three dates were picked.

✳ ✳ ✳ ✳ ✳ ✳ ✳ ✳ ✳ ✳

Teacher Script

Calendars are a great prop to use for some very puzzling magic tricks. That's because calendars are arranged in an orderly fashion. The numbers are in numerical order, and numbers above and below each other are exactly seven numbers apart. *(Demonstrate these facts on a calendar.)*

Do you remember when we practiced adding three evenly spaced numbers and then dividing our answer by 3? Do you remember what our answer was? *(Pause)* Yes, it always turned out to be the middle of the three numbers. *(Demonstrate or have a student show how the process is done.)*

What did we do to make it seem as if there were three numbers all the same instead of three evenly spaced numbers? Yes, we subtracted the difference between the numbers from the largest number and added it to the smallest number. *(Demonstrate or have a student show how the process is done.)* Knowing how to do these operations is going to help us do some very tricky tricks.

🌼 **MAY** 🌼					1	2
3	4	5	6	7	8	9
10	11	12	13	14	15	16
17	18	19	20	21	22	23
24	25	26	27	28	29	30
31						

The tricks we are going to learn will be easy for you to do, but they will amaze your audience. All we will use for these tricks is a calendar large enough so that the audience can read the numbers and a paper we can place over the calendar so that only nine numbers, three rows of three numbers each, show.

We will be able to add opposite numbers on a calendar after being told only the first number, add three columns of three numbers on a calendar knowing only one of the numbers, and know which three numbers someone has picked after being told the sum of the numbers.

Calendar Opposites: Addition and Doubling

Say: I will add four pairs of opposite numbers on a calendar without knowing what the numbers are.

THE PROPS

a few pieces of transparent tape

calendar showing one month taped or hung where the audience can see it

piece of paper with a box cut out to show three rows of three numbers each when placed over the calendar

Figure 2.1 Calendar Setup

THE TRICK

1. Hang the calendar where the audience can see it and give the cutout paper to a volunteer. Then put on your blindfold.

2. Say: **Tape the paper anywhere over the calendar so three rows of three numbers show. Tell me the first number in the box, and I will tell you the sum of each pair of opposite numbers in the box.**

3. As soon as the person tells you the first number, add 8 to it. Then double the answer. That number will be the sum of each pair of opposite numbers.

4. Say some magic words and tell your audience what your answer is.

5. Ask someone to add all the opposite pairs to prove you are right. Don't worry, you will be!

THE MAGIC

Because there are seven days in a week, numbers above and below each other on a calendar are always seven numbers apart. Adding 8 to the first number brings you one row down and one space over to the center number of the square. Once you know the center number, you double it because the center number doubled is the sum of each pair of opposite numbers.

Example:

In a calendar box showing:

7	8	9
14	15	16
21	22	23

7 is the first number.

7 + 8 = 15, the center number of the square, and 15 doubled is 30.

Look at the opposite numbers and add them.

7 + 23 = 30, 8 + 22 = 30, 9 + 21 = 30, and 14 + 16 = ? Is it 30?

Yes, because doubling the middle number of the square will always give you the sum of the opposite numbers!

Why does this work?

This works because the three numbers in any calendar row, horizontal (sideways), vertical (up and down), or diagonal (on a slant), can be added, then divided by 3 to give you the middle number. It also will give you what the other two numbers would be if you evened them out by subtracting the difference between them from the largest number and adding it to the smallest number. It is like having three numbers all the same as the middle number!

Prove to yourself that it works. Look at a calendar and choose three Sundays right in a row. Add their dates and divide your answer by 3. Did you come out with the middle number? If you added three of the middle number, would you come out with the sum of the three numbers?

Example:

If the dates were 7, 14, and 21, the sum of those numbers would be 42.

7 + 14 + 21 = 42.

42 ÷3 = 14, the middle number!

14 + 14 +14 = 42.

And 14 + 14 = 28, the sum of the two opposite numbers.

Doubling the middle number (14) is just like adding the two opposite numbers.

Calendar Opposites: Addition and Doubling

Name _____ Date _____

Now you try it:

1. On the calendar page shown, choose and circle any box of three numbers down and three numbers across.

2. Add 8 to the first number in the box and then double that number.

3. Is your answer the sum of each pair of opposite numbers? It absolutely, positively should be!

February ♥ ♥

1	2	3	4	5	6	7
8	9	10	11	12	13	14
15	16	17	18	19	20	21
22	23	24	25	26	27	28
29						

How did you do?

Materials (What props did you use?)

Procedure (How did you do the trick?)

Conclusion (What makes the magic work?)

Equations (What equations did you use to make the trick work?)

Ups and Downs: Multiplication with a One-Digit and Two-Digit Number; Simple Addition and Subtraction

Say: **Now I will add three columns of three numbers each without even looking at the numbers! And I will get the right answer every time!**

THE PROPS

a few pieces of transparent tape

small pad and pencil for you to record your answers

calendar and a paper to lay over the calendar so that only three rows of three numbers each show

THE TRICK

1. Choose a volunteer, point out the paper and the calendar, and turn your back to the volunteer. You might want to use a pad and pencil to record your answers.
2. Say: **Tape the paper over the calendar so that three rows of three numbers each are showing. Tell me the center number and I will tell you the sum of each column of numbers in the square.**
3. When the person tells you the center number, multiply it by 3 to get the sum of the middle column. Write down that number.
4. Subtract 3 from that answer to get the sum of the first column. Write that down too.
5. Add 3 to your first answer to get the sum of the third column. Say some magic words, then say the sum of each column of three numbers.
6. Ask someone from the audience to add each column to prove you are right! Don't worry. You will be!

THE MAGIC

Whenever you multiply the center number by 3, you will get the sum of the center column. By adding 3 to that number, you get the sum of the last column of numbers. By subtracting 3 from the center sum, you get the sum of the first column.

Example:

13	14	15
20	21	22
27	28	29

First multiply the center number by 3 to get the sum of the center column.

The center number is 21, and 3 × 21 = 63. Now you know that the sum of that column is 63 (14 + 21 + 28 = 63).

Because there are 3 numbers, each one less than the number after it, you subtract 3 from 63 to get 60 for the sum of the first column (13 + 20 + 27 = 60).

Because there are 3 numbers, each one more than the numbers they follow, you add 3 to 63 to make 66 for the sum of the last column (15 + 22 + 29 = 66).

The three sums are 60, 63, and 66.

Why does this work?

Just as in the last trick, this works because the numbers above and below each other on a calendar are evenly spaced, seven numbers apart. The top number is 7 less than the center number, and the bottom number is 7 more than the center number. If you take 7 away from the bottom number and add it to the top number, you have three all the same as the center number! Adding three of the same numbers together is the same as multiplying one of them by 3 to get the sum of the column.

Example:

7

14

21

14 × 3 = 42 and 7 + 14 + 21 = 42

Once you know the sum of the middle column, it's easy to find the other two answers. Numbers on a calendar are in numerical order so column one, because it has three numbers, will be 3 less and column three, with three numbers also, will be 3 more. Easy when you know how, isn't it?

Ups and Downs: Multiplication with a One-Digit and Two-Digit Number; Simple Addition and Subtraction

Name _____ Date _____

Now you try it:

You might want to use a pad and pencil to write your answers as you "magically" discover them. Being a magician doesn't mean you can't forget things.

1. On the calendar below, choose and circle any box of three numbers down and three numbers across.
2. Multiply the center number by 3.
3. Subtract 3 from that number to get the sum of the first column.
4. Add 3 to your first answer to get the sum of the third column.

february ♥ ♥

1	2	3	4	5	6	7
8	9	10	11	12	13	14
15	16	17	18	19	20	21
22	23	24	25	26	27	28
29						

How did you do?

Materials (What props did you use?)

Procedure (How did you do the trick?)

Conclusion (What makes the magic work?)

Equations (What equations did you use to make the trick work?)

Dates, Dates Everywhere: Simple Division, Addition, and Subtraction

Say: **Without looking, I will be able to tell what three numbers you pick from a calendar.**

THE PROPS

crayon

page from a calendar

THE TRICK

1. Give a volunteer the calendar page and the crayon.
2. Turn your back or put on your blindfold.
3. Say: **Circle any three dates in a row. Add those three numbers and tell me the sum. I will then tell you the three numbers you picked.**
4. Divide the number the volunteer gives you by 3. That number and the number right before it and the number right after it are the 3 numbers they picked.
5. Say some magic words and tell the person what three numbers she chose.

THE MAGIC

The volunteer gives you the sum of the numbers. You divide that number by 3 and discover the middle number. The other two numbers the volunteer chose are the numbers right before and right after the middle one.

Example:

Use the numbers 9, 10, and 11.

9 + 10 + 11 = 30.

30 ÷ 3 = 10, the middle number.

1 less than 10 is 9 (10 - 1 = 9) and 1 more than 10 is 11 (10 + 1 = 11).

Why does this work?

This trick works because the numbers on the calendar are in numerical order. The volunteer picks three numbers in order, adds them and tells you the sum. When you divide the sum of three numbers in numerical order by the number 3, the answer will be the middle number. Because the numbers are in order, the number before the middle number and the number after it are the correct three dates.

This trick works when your volunteers pick any *odd amount of numbers*. If they pick five numbers, you divide by the number 5. The answer and the two numbers right before it and the two numbers right after it are the five numbers they picked. *(Demonstrate or have a student work through the process.)* If they pick seven numbers, you divide by the number 7 and tell them that number and the three numbers right before and right after it. Try it and see for yourself. *(Demonstrate or have a student work through the process.)*

Dates, Dates Everywhere: Simple Division, Addition, and Subtraction

Name _____ Date _____

Now you try it:

1. Circle three consecutive numbers on the calendar shown.
2. Add those numbers and divide the answer by 3.
3. That number should be the middle number of the three numbers you picked. That's because, when you divide the sum of three consecutive numbers by the number 3, the answer will always be the middle number.
4. Subtract one to get the number before and add one to get the number after.

How did you do?

Materials (What props did you use?)

Procedure (How did you do the trick?)

Conclusion (What makes the magic work?)

Equations (What equations did you use to make the trick work?)

Chapter III
DICE DOINGS

✳ ✳ ✳ ✳ ✳ ✳ ✳ ✳ ✳ ✳

Teacher Notes

Ordinary dice are used for all the tricks in this chapter. The math in these four tricks is simple, and the reasoning is easy to grasp.

Trick 1. Transparent Dice: Simple Addition and Subtraction

The magician will be able to add the numbers on the bottoms of dice without looking at them. Although this trick calls for four dice, any number of dice can be used; instructions are provided at the end of the trick for changing the number used.

Trick 2. Magic Dice: Simple Multiplication, Addition, and Subtraction

Without looking, the magician will be able to tell which two numbers have been rolled on a pair of dice.

Trick 3. Roll 'Em, Partner: Doubling and Halving Numbers, and Simple Subtraction

A number is chosen secretly and changed by doubling and addition and subtraction. The magician will say the answer.

Trick 4. I've Got Your Number: Doubling, Simple Division, and Subtraction

The magician will be able to tell which number is rolled on one die. This trick also can be done without dice, so it's like having two tricks in one. Do it once with dice and once without. It works equally well either way.

✳ ✳ ✳ ✳ ✳ ✳ ✳ ✳ ✳ ✳

Teacher Script

You've probably played a lot of games in which you used dice. Well, in the next few tricks you will be using dice again, but this time you will be performing magic tricks with the dice. The dice will be ordinary ones, just like you use in your games, but the tricks won't be ordinary at all.

You will be able to add the numbers on the bottoms of dice without seeing them, tell which one or two numbers have been rolled, and know what the answer is after a number has been changed in several ways.

Some of the following tricks call for using paper and marker. Just as you did in some of the tricks you've already learned, you should have the volunteer work on a large piece of paper that the audience can see.

Now it's time to toss those little cubes and see what magic we can roll!

Transparent Dice:
Simple Addition and Subtraction

Say: **I will add the numbers on the bottom of the dice even though I can't see them!**

THE PROPS

four dice

THE TRICK

1. Ask a volunteer to toss the four dice on the table.

2. Say: **With my magical powers, I am able to see through the dice. I will add the numbers on the bottom of these dice, even though I cannot see them.**

3. In your head, add the numbers on the top of the dice and subtract that number from 28. Say the answer out loud.

4. Ask the volunteer to turn over the dice, one at a time, and add the bottom numbers out loud so the audience can hear. The sum will be the number you have named!

THE MAGIC

If you use four dice, all you have to do is subtract the sum of the numbers on the top of the dice from 28 to find the sum of the numbers on the bottom of the dice.

Why does this work?

When you add the number on the top and bottom on any one die, the answer will be 7. If you have four dice, that is 4 times 7, or 28. 28 is the sum of the top and bottom numbers on all four dice. By subtracting the sum of the top numbers from 28, you will always come out with the sum of the bottom numbers.

Example:

If the sum of the top numbers on the dice equals 11, then 28 – 11 = 17, which is what the bottom numbers will add up to.

You can use any number of dice you like. Just remember that the sum of the top and bottom numbers on each die equals 7. So, if you use two dice, multiply 7 times 2 to get 14 and subtract the top numbers from 14. If you use three dice, multiply 7 times 3 to get 21 and subtract the top numbers from 21. If you use five dice, multiply 7 times 5 to get 35 and subtract the top sum from 35. What should you do if you use six dice?

Transparent Dice:
Simple Addition and Subtraction

Name _____ Date _____

Now you try it:

1. Roll four dice and add the numbers that are on top.
2. Subtract your answer from 28 and write down that number.
3. Add up the numbers on the bottoms of the dice.
4. Is it the same number you arrived at when you did your subtraction? Of course it is.

This trick will always work for you because when you add the number on the top and bottom of any one die, the answer will be 7. You used four dice, and $4 \times 7 = 28$. When you subtracted the sum of the top numbers from 28, you arrived at the sum of the bottom numbers.

How did you do?

Materials (What props did you use?)

Procedure (How did you do the trick?)

Conclusion (What makes the magic work?)

Equations (What equations did you use to make the trick work?)

Magic Dice: Simple Multiplication, Addition, and Subtraction

Say: **I won't look but I will know which two numbers come up when you roll dice!**

THE PROPS

two dice, a large piece of paper, and dark-colored marker

THE TRICK

1. Put the paper where the audience can see it, and give a volunteer the dice and marker.
2. Turn your back or use your blindfold.
3. Say: **Roll two dice and write down the numbers.**
4. Say: **Pick one of the numbers and multiply it by 5.**
5. Say: **Add 7 to the product (the answer).**
6. Say: **Now double that answer.**
7. Say: **Now add the number on the other die and tell me the answer.**
8. In your head, subtract 14 from the number the person tells you, then tell the person the two digits in your answer. They will be the two numbers the volunteer rolled.

THE MAGIC

When you multiply one of the numbers by 5, double the answer, and add the other number, you end up with the two numbers rolled. You use the number 7 to confuse the audience.

Why does this work?

This works because multiplying a number by 5 and then doubling it is just like multiplying it by 10.

Example:

$3 \times 5 = 15$ and 15 doubled is 30

$3 \times 10 = 30$

When you multiply a number by 10, you always get the same number with a 0 after it. For instance, $2 \times 10 = 20$ is the same as 2 with a 0 after it; $3 \times 10 = 30$ is 3 with a 0 after it.

The volunteer multiplies one of the numbers by five and then doubles it. Since 5 times 2 equals 10, that's the same as multiplying it by 10. That gives you the first number the person rolled with a 0 after it. Then the person added the second number, and you now have the two numbers he rolled. The 7 is added just to fool the audience.

In step five you told the volunteer to add 7 to the product, then had him double that number in the next step. When you double 7, you get 14, so when you subtract 14, you are just taking out what the person put in and you end up with the two numbers he rolled.

Actually you can use any number you want in step five as long as you subtract twice that amount to get the answer. For example, if you tell the person to add 6 to the product, just remember to subtract 12.

Magic Dice: Simple Multiplication, Addition, and Subtraction

Name _____ Date _____

Now you try it:

1. Roll two dice. Write the two numbers you rolled.

2. Multiple one of the numbers you rolled by 5.

3. Add 7 to the product.

4. Double the answer.

5. Add the number on the other die.

6. Subtract 14 from your answer. Did you end up with the two numbers you rolled in the first place?

How did you do?

Materials (What props did you use?)

Procedure (How did you do the trick?)

Conclusion (What makes the magic work?)

Equations (What equations did you use to make the trick work?)

Roll 'Em, Partner: Doubling and Halving Numbers, and Simple Subtraction

Say: **After you roll a number and change it by doubling it and adding and subtracting other numbers, I will tell you what your answer is without looking.**

THE PROPS

dark -colored marker

large piece of paper

one die

THE TRICK

1. Put the paper where the audience can see it and give a volunteer the marker.
2. Turn your back or put on your blindfold.
3. Say: **I am going to ask you to do some work with numbers. Please use the paper and marker to help you follow my directions.**
4. Say: **Roll the die and double the number on top of the die.**
5. Now, in your head, *you* pick an *even* number between 2 and 10. (2, 4, 6, 8, 10).

   (IMPORTANT: Be sure to remember this number!)

   Say: **Add_____(the number you picked) to your answer.**
6. Say: **Now divide your new answer in half.**
7. Say: **Subtract the number that you rolled on the die.**
8. Say some magic words and tell the answer. It will be half the even number you gave in step five.

THE MAGIC

The answer will always be one half of the even number you chose in step five.

Why does this work?

This works because when the volunteer doubles the number on the die and divides it in half, she ends up with the number on the die.

Example:

2 doubled is 4 (2 × 2 = 4).

Half of 4 is 2 (4 ÷2 = 2).

So when the volunteer subtracts her number from the answer in step 7, all she is left with is half of the number you gave her because your number was divided in half, too!

Roll 'Em, Partner: Doubling and Halving Numbers, and Simple Subtraction

Name _____ Date _____

Now you try it:

1. Roll one die. Write the number you rolled.
2. Double the number.
3. Pick an even number from 2 through 10 and add it to the answer.
4. Divide the new answer in half.
5. Subtract the number you rolled.
6. The answer will always be half of the even number you choose. Simple as can be when you know what you're doing. Right?

How did you do?

Materials (What props did you use?)

Procedure (How did you do the trick?)

Conclusion (What makes the magic work?)

Equations (What equations did you use to make the trick work?)

I've Got Your Number: Doubling, Simple Division, and Subtraction

Say: **Without looking, I will correctly guess what number you roll on one die.**

THE PROPS

dark-colored marker

piece of paper

one die

THE TRICK

1. Put the paper where the audience can see it and give a volunteer the marker and a die.
2. Turn your back on the volunteer or put on your blindfold.
3. Say: **Roll a number and write it on the piece of paper. Don't tell me what you wrote.**
4. Say: **Double the number you rolled and add 2 to the answer.**
5. Say: **Divide that number by 2 and tell me your final answer.**
6. Subtract 1 from the volunteer's answer to get the number he started with.
7. Announce that number and take a deep bow.

THE MAGIC

All you have to do in this trick is ask someone to double the number he rolled on one die, add 2, then divide the answer by 2. You subtract 1 from the answer he tells you, and you will know what number he rolled.

After you have practiced this trick for a while, you can change it by choosing a different even number to add. The magic works when you subtract half of whatever number you say to add. For example, if you choose a 4, you would subtract half of 4 (2) from the final answer. If you choose 6, you would subtract 3, and so on.

You also can do this trick without using dice. Ask the volunteer to pick any number as high or as low as he wants. Since the magic depends on the number you choose, it will always work no matter what number the person picks, even if he picks one million.

Why does this work?

When the person doubles his number and then divides it by 2, he is really doubling it and then splitting it in half. This gives him the number he rolled in the first place! This is like walking the same number of steps forwards and then backwards. He ends up in the same place he started. Since he split the number you gave him (2) in half, too, you subtract half of 2 (1) and end up with the number he rolled.

Example:

Roll a 6.

Double 6 to get 12 ($6 \times 2 = 12$).

Add 2, which equals 14 ($12 + 2 = 14$).

Divide that number by 2, which equals 7 ($14 \div 2 = 7$)

Subtract 1 and you are back at the number you rolled, 6 ($7 - 1 = 6$).

DICE DOINGS Trick 4 Student Handout

I've Got Your Number: Doubling, Simple Division, and Subtraction

Name _____ Date _____

Now you try it:

1. Roll a die. Write the number here.
2. Double the number you rolled.
3. Add 2 to the answer.
4. Divide that number in half.
5. Subtract 1 and end up with the number you rolled in the first step. TA-DA!

Remember when you double a number and then divide it in half, you end up with the number you began with. In this trick you added a 2 to the number that was rolled. When the answer was divided in half, the 2 you added was split in half along with the number you rolled on the die. Half of 2 is 1. If you add a different number, just subtract half of that number and you will have the correct answer. Pretty tricky, don't you think?

How did you do?

Materials (What props did you use?)

Procedure (How did you do the trick?)

Conclusion (What makes the magic work?)

Equations (What equations did you use to make the trick work?)

Chapter IV
MONEY MADNESS
✶ ✶ ✶ ✶ ✶ ✶ ✶ ✶ ✶ ✶
Teacher Notes

As in the preceding chapter, the math computation in the tricks in this chapter is not difficult, but the reasoning in two of the tricks is more challenging. For all of the tricks except number 4, Heads or Tails, any small objects can be used if coins are not available.

To give the audience a good view of what is happening in the trick, use an overhead projector for tricks 1, 2, 3 and 5. You probably will want to use a piece of clear plastic over the glass of the projector to protect it from scratches.

Trick 1. Evening the Odds: Simple Addition, Even and Odd Numbers (easy reasoning)
An even number of coins will be turned into an odd number, and an odd number of coins will be turned into an even number.

Trick 2. Leftovers, Anyone? Simple Subtraction (several steps but easy reasoning)
Without looking, the magician will be able to tell how many coins are left after some have been taken away.

Trick 3. Hidden Coins: Simple Addition, Subtraction (easy reasoning)
A volunteer moves coins in three separate steps. Without looking, the magician knows exactly how many coins the person is hiding.

Trick 4. Heads or Tails: Logic (challenging reasoning)
The magician will tell whether a hidden coin is turned heads-up or tails-up. Coins or any object that has two distinctly different sides must be used in this trick. If using coins, newer coins are best, as it is easier to see whether heads or tails is turned up.

Trick 5. Share Magic: Doubling and Simple Multiplication (challenging reasoning)
Two volunteers share their coins, and the magician will know how many coins one of them has. This trick calls for 50 to 60 coins, but anything can be used instead: counters, buttons, rocks, and candy. To use an overhead with this trick, place the objects on a nearby table and ask the two volunteers to place whatever number of objects they move onto the overhead so the audience can see them.

Trick 6. Spare Change, Anyone? Addition, Subtraction, and Multiplication of Up to Four-Digit Numbers (challenging reasoning)
The magician will tell the volunteer's age and how much spare change has been secretly added to that number.

✳ ✳ ✳ ✳ ✳ ✳ ✳ ✳ ✳ ✳

Teacher Script

You're going to learn some tricks using money, but even though these tricks call for using coins, they work just as well with buttons, stones, or checkers. We'll use whatever is handy.

We will need some shiny pennies for one of the tricks called Heads or Tails because you have to see the heads and tails clearly in order for the trick to work. In this trick, you'll be able to tell whether the coin someone is hiding has its tail or its head showing. In one other trick, Spare Change, you'll need to choose volunteers who have some spare change so you can magically tell them how much money they have without ever looking at the coins.

In tricks 1, 2, 3, and 5, we might be using an overhead projector so that everyone can see what is happening with the coins. These tricks involve laying coins on a table. It will be easier for the audience to know what is happening if they see what you're doing projected on a wall.

So, on to Money Madness!

Evening the Odds: Simple Addition, Even and Odd Numbers

Say: **I can turn an odd number of coins into an even number or an even number of coins into an odd number!**

THE PROPS

20 or more coins

overhead projector

THE TRICK

1. Lay out the coins on the table or projector.
2. Pick up an *odd* number of coins and hold them in your hand. Choose a volunteer, then turn your back.
3. Say: **Now you take away as many coins as you want.**
4. Say: **If you have left an odd number of coins, I will turn them into an even number with the coins I picked. If you have left an even number of coins, I will turn them into an odd number.**
5. Ask the volunteer to count the coins left on the projector and tell whether the number of coins is even or odd.
6. Open your hand and add your coins to the coins on the projector. If the volunteer had left an even number of coins, the number will now be odd. If the volunteer had left an odd number, the number will now be even.

THE MAGIC

If you make sure you have an odd number of coins in your hand, you will always be able to change an odd number into an even number or an even number into an odd number.

Why does this work?

You are holding an odd number of coins in your hand. An odd number added to an even number always comes out odd. An odd number added to an odd number always comes out even.

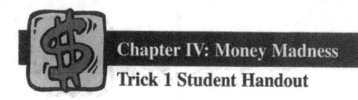

Evening the Odds: Simple Addition, Even and Odd Numbers

Name _____ Date _____

Now you try it:

To change an even number to an odd number:

1. Hold an odd number of coins in your hand.

2. Lay out an even number of coins on a table or on your desk.

3. Add the coins from your hand to those you have laid out. The total number of coins will be odd.

To change an odd number to an even number:

1. Hold an odd number of coins in your hand.

2. Lay out an odd number of coins on a table or on your desk.

3. Add the coins from your hand to those you have laid out. The total number of coins will be even.

Remember: An odd number added to an even number always comes out odd.

An odd number added to an odd number always comes out even.

How did you do?

Materials (What props did you use?)

Procedure (How did you do the trick?)

Conclusion (What makes the magic work?)

Equations (What equations did you use to make the trick work?)

Leftovers, Anyone? Simple Subtraction

Say: **Without looking, I will tell you how many pennies are left on the table after you take some away.**

THE PROPS

any *even* number of coins above 20

overhead projector

THE TRICK

1. Give a volunteer an *even* number of pennies.
2. Turn your back or put on your blindfold.
3. Say: **Make two rows of pennies with the same number of pennies in each row.**
4. Say: **Now take one penny from the bottom row.**
5. Say: **Take as many pennies from the top row as you want. Tell me how many you took.**
   (*IMPORTANT: Be sure to remember this number!*)
6. Say: **Count how many pennies are left in the top row. Take that many pennies from the bottom row.**
7. Say: **Now take away all the pennies from the top row.**
8. The volunteer tells you how many pennies she took from the top row in step five
9. Subtract 1 from the number she gives you. That is how many pennies are left.
10. Say some magic words and then announce how many pennies are left.

THE MAGIC

Follow the directions exactly, step by step, and you will always know how many coins are left on the table.

Why does this work?

This trick works because, one step at a time, the volunteer takes all the pennies away except for the number she told you in step 5 minus the one penny she took away in the first step.

Figure 4.1 Steps in Performing Leftovers, Anyone?

Step 1: Make two rows of pennies with the same number in each row.

Step 2: Take one penny from the bottom row.

Step 3: Take as many pennies from the top row as you want (for example, three).

Step 4: Count how many are left in the top row and take that many from the bottom row.

Step 5: Take away all the pennies in the top row.

Result: You are left with two pennies, which is one less than the volunteer took away in step three.

Leftovers, Anyone? Simple Subtraction

Name _____ Date _____

Now you try it:

1. Make two equal rows of pennies.
2. Take one penny from the bottom row.
3. Take as many as you want from the top row. *Remember this number. Write it down if you want to.*
4. Count how many pennies are left in the top row and take that many away from the bottom row.
5. Take all the pennies away from the top row.
6. How many are left? If you followed the instructions exactly, there should be one less than the number you wrote down. Aren't numbers great? They make magic tricks so easy to do!

How did you do?

Materials (What props did you use?)

Procedure (How did you do the trick?)

Conclusion (What makes the magic work?)

Equations (What equations did you use to make the trick work?)

Hidden Coins: Simple Addition, Subtraction

Say: **I will correctly guess how many coins are in someone's hand.**

THE PROPS

20 coins

overhead projector

THE TRICK

1. Lay out the 20 coins on the overhead projector.
2. Turn your back and ask a volunteer to take any number of coins from 1 to 9 and put them in an empty pocket.
3. Say: **Count how many coins are left and add the two digits of that number.** (For example, if 15 are left, he will add 1 and 5 to make 6.)
4. Say: **Take that number of coins and put them in your pocket, too.**
5. Say: **Now take any number of coins and hide them in your hand.**
6. Turn around, count how many coins are left on the projector, and subtract that number from 9.
7. Your answer is the number of coins in the volunteer's hand. If no coins are left, the volunteer is holding 9 coins. If 9 coins are left, the volunteer's hand is empty.

THE MAGIC

The number of coins in the person's pocket will always be 11 no matter how many coins are taken at first. The sum of the digits of the remaining coins added to the number taken from the overhead projector will always equal 11.

Example:

$20 - 3 = 17$ (the volunteer takes away 3 coins).

$1 + 7 = 8$ (the volunteer adds the digits of the number of coins left, 17).

$8 + 3 = 11$ (that sum [8] added to the number taken [3] is 11).

If you don't believe me, try it with all the numbers from 1 to 9 and see. Because 20 minus 11 equals 9, there will be 9 coins left until the person takes some to hold in his hand. By subtracting the number of coins remaining on the overhead projector from 9, you discover how many coins he is holding in his hand.

Why does this work?

Nine is a very tricky number. In fact, this book has a chapter that will tell you more about the mystifying 9. In this trick no matter how many coins are taken in the first place, there will be 9 coins left on the table. So if there are not 9 coins left, all you have to do is figure out how many are missing, and that's how many are in the volunteer's hand. You do that by subtracting the number of coins left from 9. Your answer will be how many coins hidden in someone's hand.

Example:

Lay out 20 coins on a table.

Take any number of coins and put them in your pocket. Let's say you take 6 coins.

Count the number of coins left (14) and add those two digits together (1 + 4 = 5).

Take that many coins and put them in your pocket too.

You should have 11 coins in your pocket and 9 left on the table.

You will always know how many coins are now taken because you know there should be 9 left.

Hidden Coins:
Simple Addition, Subtraction

Name _____ Date _____

Now you try it:

1. Ask a friend to practice this trick with you.

2. Lay out 20 coins on a table. Close your eyes.

3. Ask your friend to take any number of coins from 1 to 9 and put them in his pocket.

4. Tell him to count the number of coins left and add the two digits in that number together.

5. Tell him to take that many coins and put them in his pocket, too. There should be nine coins left on the table.

6. Tell him to take as many coins as he wants and hold them in his hand.

7. You can see that you will always know how many coins he took because you know there should be 9 left. If there are not 9 left, subtract the number of coins on the table from 9 to find out how many coins your friend is hiding. If there are 9 coins left, then your friend did not take any coins. If there are no coins left, then your friend took 9 coins (all of them).

How did you do?

Materials (What props did you use?)

Procedure (How did you do the trick?)

Conclusion (What makes the magic work?)

Equations (What equations did you use to make the trick work?)

Heads or Tails: Logic

Say: **I will be able to tell you whether you are hiding a heads-up or a tails-up coin without looking.**

THE PROPS

Several coins arranged on a table with some heads-up and some tails-up

(Note: You cannot use anything but coins for this trick.)

THE TRICK

1. Lay out any number of coins on the table. Some of the coins should be tails-up and some should be heads-up.

2. Count to yourself how many coins are heads-up.

2. Turn your back and ask a volunteer to turn over as many coins as she wants, one coin at a time.

3. Say: **Each time you turn a coin over, call out "Turn."**

4. Each time the volunteer calls out the word *turn,* add one to the number of heads-up coins you counted (do this silently, to yourself).

5. When she is done, say: **Cover up one coin with your hand.**

6. Turn around and count how many heads-up coins are showing.

   a. If the number you counted in your head came out even and the number of heads-up coins showing is even, the hidden coin is tails-up. **Remember: Even and Even = Tails-Up**

   b. If the number you counted in your head came out odd and the number of heads-up coins showing is odd, the hidden coin is tails-up. **Remember: Odd and Odd = Tails-Up**

   c. If the number of coins you counted in your head came out even and the number of heads-up coins showing is odd, the hidden coin is heads-up. **Remember: Even and Odd = Heads-Up**

   d. If the number of coins you counted in your head came out odd and the number of heads-up coins showing is even, the hidden coin is heads-up. **Remember: Odd and Even = Heads-Up**

7. Say some magic words and tell the volunteer whether the hidden coin is tails-up or heads-up.

THE MAGIC

The magic in this trick comes from plain old counting! You count the number of heads-up coins before you put on your blindfold. Each time you hear the word *turn,* you add one to that total. The number you reach will tell you whether an odd or an even number of head-up coins are showing on the table.

Why does this work?

If the number you have reached is even, an even number of coins should be heads-up. If the number you have reached is odd, an odd number of coins should be heads-up. This trick works because each time a coin is turned, the number of heads-up coins is changed. We don't care *how many* heads-up coins are showing. All that matters is whether *an even or an odd number* of heads-up coins are showing. You add the number of times a coin has been turned to the number of heads-up coins you counted in the first place. That number tells you whether you should have an even or an odd number of heads-up coins. It's logic, or what makes sense!

Heads or Tails: Logic

Name _____ Date _____

Now you try it:

1. Ask a friend to practice this trick with you.
2. Arrange 10 coins on a table with some tails and some heads showing.
3. Count the number of heads-up coins. Remember that number.
4. Now ask someone to turn over a few coins and say "Turn" each time she does.
5. Add one to the beginning number each time she tells you a coin is turned.
6. Remember whether you end up with an *even* number or an *odd* number.
7. If you ended up with an *even* number, you know that the number of heads-up coins showing should be even. If you ended up with an *odd* number, you know that the number of heads-up coins showing should be odd.

How did you do?

Materials (What props did you use?)

Procedure (How did you do the trick?)

Conclusion (What makes the magic work?)

Equations (What equations did you use to make the trick work?)

Share Magic:
Doubling and Simple Multiplication

In this trick you will use two volunteers. You will be able to tell how many coins one has left after sharing with the other volunteer.

Say: **We all know that it's nice to share. Today one of you is going to share what you have with someone else. I will be able to tell what one of you has left after you do.**

THE PROPS

70 coins (or rocks or dried beans) in a bowl

overhead projector with a line drawn down the middle to make two separate sides

THE TRICK

1. Ask for two volunteers. If you don't know their names, tell them they will be called A and B. Ask the volunteers to stand one on either side of the projector. Put on your blindfold.

2. Say: **A, please take from 10 to 20 coins from the bowl and put them on your side of the projector.**

3. Say: **B, please double that number and take that many coins from the bowl and put them on your side of the projector.**

4. Say: **Now, A, it's time to share. Give 5 of your coins to B.**

5. Say: **B, now it's your turn to share. Count how many A has left and give A twice that many from your coins.**

6. Rub your head and say some magic words before you multiply the number you told A to give to B (5) by 3 and tell them that B has 15 coins left.

THE MAGIC

This is a trick that you can do as often as you like because the answer depends on the number you tell A to share. By changing that number you will always come out with a different answer.

Trick 5

Why does this work?

To understand this trick we have to think of the coins each volunteer takes as a pile of coins.

Example:

A takes 10 coins and B takes twice that amount (20).

Now A has one pile of 10 coins and B has two piles of 10 coins each.

So there are three equal piles.

A  B

Then A gives B the part of his pile you tell him to give. Let's say it is 4 coins.

A  B

B now counts how many coins A has (It is 6 because 10 − 4 = 6) and gives back twice that amount. B gives A 12 coins because 2 × 6 = 12.

A

Now B is left with three piles, but there are only 4 coins in each pile. He had to take 6 from each of his piles of 10 to give to A. Because 3 × 4 = 12, B is left with 12 coins.

B

Share Magic:
Doubling and Simple Multiplication

Name _____ Date _____

Now you try it:

1. Ask a friend to practice this trick with you.
2. Lay out 70 coins or other objects.
3. Pick any numbers of coins from 10 to 20 and put them in your pile.
4. Ask your partner to take double that amount and put them in his pile.
5. How many will you share? Let's say 4.
6. Give your partner 4 of your coins.
7. Tell your partner to give you double the amount that you have left.
8. How many is your partner left with? Your partner should have 12.
9. Multiply the number you shared by 3.
10. Three times 4 (the number of coins you shared) equals 12 ($3 \times 4 = 12$).

Remember: The only number that matters in this trick is how many coins you tell A to share.

How did you do?

Materials (What props did you use?)

Procedure (How did you do the trick?)

Conclusion (What makes the magic work?)

Equations (What equations did you use to make the trick work?)

Spare Change, Anyone?
Addition, Subtraction, and Multiplication of Up to Four-Digit Numbers

Say: **In this trick, by using my magic powers I will be able to tell you your age and how much spare change you have in your pocket.**

THE PROPS

dark-colored marker

large piece of paper

volunteer who has spare change that is less than one dollar

calculator for the volunteer

piece of paper and a pencil (optional)

THE TRICK

1. Ask for a volunteer who has spare change that is less than one dollar.
2. Put on your blindfold and ask the volunteer to write her age on the paper.
3. Say: **Now multiply your age by 2 and add 5 to the answer.**
4. Say: **Here's a hard part. Multiply that answer by 50.**
5. Say: **Do you know how many days there are in a year? There are 365. Subtract 365 from your answer.**
6. Say: **Now take out your spare change from your pocket and count it. It should be less than one dollar. Add the amount of money to your last answer.**
7. Say: **Tell me your final answer, and I will tell you how old you are and how much change you had in your pocket.**
8. When the volunteer tells you the final answer, add 115 to that number in your head or use a pencil and a piece of paper. The four numbers you end up with will tell you the person's age and the amount of change in that order.

THE MAGIC

By adding 115 to the final answer you will always get four digits. The first two digits will be the person's age, and the second two will be the amount of money the volunteer had.

If the volunteer is younger than 10 years old, the first number will be the age, and the second two numbers will be the amount of money.

Why does this work?

This trick will work only if the steps are followed exactly as they are given and you remember the important number of 115. How do we get the number 115? In steps three and four, the volunteer adds 5 and multiplies the answer by 50 ($5 \times 50 = 250$). This step adds 250 to the answer. Next 365 is subtracted from the answer. 250 is 115 less than 365 ($250 + 115 = 365$). You need to add 115 to the final answer to make up the 365 the volunteer subtracted. At the end of the trick, you add 115 from the answer given to you and end up with the volunteer's age and the amount of change she added to the mix!

Example:

Say your volunteer is 50.

$50 \times 2 = 100$

$100 + 5 = 105$

$105 \times 50 = 5250$

$5250 - 365 = 4885$

Now the volunteer adds 37 cents to the total ($4885 + 37 = 4922$).

You secretly add 115 and come up with 5037 ($4922 + 115 = 5037$).

50 in the volunteer's age, and 37 is the amount of money added in.

Pretty slick, isn't it? Follow the steps carefully, remember the number 115, and you will never fail at this trick!

Spare Change, Anyone? Addition, Subtraction, and Multiplication of Up to Four-Digit Numbers

Name _____ Date _____

Now you try it:

1. Write your age and multiply it by 2.

2. Add 5 and multiply the answer by 50.

3. Subtract 365 and add your change to the answer.

4. Add 115 and you should have four digits.

5. The first two digits are your age and the last two are the amount of money you added.

How did you do?

Materials (What props did you use?)

Procedure (How did you do the trick?)

Conclusion (What makes the magic work?)

Equations (What equations did you use to make the trick work?)

Chapter V
A LITTLE BIT OF EXTRA MAGIC
✳ ✳ ✳ ✳ ✳ ✳ ✳ ✳ ✳ ✳
Teacher Notes

Here are several tricks that don't fit into any of the categories of the first chapters. The reasoning behind Tricks 1 and 4, Do You Remember? and Magic Fingers, is very simple. While not difficult, the reasoning for the others is more involved.

Trick 1. Do You Remember? Mental Addition and Subtraction of a 15-Digit Number

The magician will be able to tell what number is missing from a series of 15 single-digit numbers after hearing them once in order and once out of order.

Trick 2. What Is Your Age? Simple Multiplication, Addition, Division, and Subtraction

The magician will guess someone's age correctly.

Trick 3. Young or Old: Addition with Carrying and Subtraction with Borrowing

Here's another way to guess someone's age. To determine the answer in this trick, the magician can use paper and pencil if necessary.

Trick 4. Magic Fingers: Trickery!

This trick involves trickery, not math. The magician writes numbers given by the audience on individual pieces of paper and puts them in a bag. When one piece of paper is drawn from the bag, the magician knows exactly what number is written on it!

Trick 5. Changeover: Addition, Subtraction, Multiplication, and Division

A secret number is chosen and changed in five different ways, but the magician will know the final number.

Trick 6. Lucky 63: Addition with Double-Digit Numbers

Six number charts are used to determine which number someone has chosen from 1 to 63. The charts that follow the final chapter are in actual size, ready to be copied and mounted on cardboard so the audience can see them clearly. Smaller versions of the number charts are included in the student directions for the trick to facilitate practice.

✳ ✳ ✳ ✳ ✳ ✳ ✳ ✳ ✳ ✳

Teacher Script

Let's talk a little about the magic tricks you've already learned. Which did you like best? Did you like working with clocks, dice, or money? Why?

Does anyone remember some of the math we did to make the magic tricks work? *(Encourage the students to talk about the equations that they used to work the magic.)*

Now you are about to learn some very tricky tricks. We won't be using many props at all, mostly just paper and marker. You will be able to memorize a string of 15 numbers in just a few minutes, learn two ways to guess someone's age correctly, guess a secret number in two different ways, and know what number someone ends up with even after they change a number in five different ways. We'll also use some number charts to guess which number someone picks from 1 to 63.

Are you ready for more magic?

Do You Remember? Mental Addition and Subtraction of a 15-Digit Number

Say: **I will memorize a 15-digit number after hearing it only one time.**

THE PROPS

dark-colored marker

large piece of paper

THE TRICK

1. Put on your blindfold and ask a volunteer to write down 15 single-digit numbers.
2. Say: **Read the numbers to me one at a time, telling me one number each time I raise my hand.**
3. As the numbers are being read, add them in your head (not out loud), keeping a running total. Don't raise your hand for a new number until you have added the last number to your total.
4. After all the numbers have been given to you, say: **Circle one number, any number you choose.**
5. Say: **Repeat all the numbers except the one you circled and I will tell you the number you left out. You can say them out of order if you want to make it harder for me, but please check each number off as you say it.**
6. Add the numbers in your head, raising your hand when you are ready for another number.
7. When the volunteer is done, reveal the number that is circled by subtracting the second sum from the first.

THE MAGIC

You only pretend to be memorizing the numbers as they are read to you. This trick is simple addition and subtraction, but the audience won't know that. It will seem to them that you must have memorized the numbers because you know which one was left out even when the numbers were given to you out of order.

Why does this work?

You add the numbers that are given to you twice. Then you subtract the smaller total from the larger one. The difference between the two numbers is the number that was circled. Let's say that the numbers given to you are 7 8 4 6 5 3 7 9 1 6 4 2 8 3 4. When you add the digits the first time, the total is 77. Suppose the volunteer circles and leaves out the first "6" digit when he reads the numbers again. This time, the sum is only 71. You know that the circled number must be 6 because 77 − 71 = 6.

Do You Remember? Mental Addition and Subtraction of a 15-Digit Number

Name _____ Date _____

Now you try it:

1. Ask a friend to practice this trick with you.
2. Close your eyes.
3. Ask your friend to write down a series of 15 single-digit numbers.
4. Add them up in your head as your friend reads them to you one by one, each time you raise your hand.
5. Ask your friend to circle one number.
6. Now ask him to read the numbers again in any order, leaving out the number he circled but checking the numbers off as he reads them.
7. Add the numbers in your head as they are read to you.
8. Subtract the second sum from the first. Your answer is the number he circled. Nothing to it, is there?

How did you do?

Materials (What props did you use?)

Procedure (How did you do the trick?)

Conclusion (What makes the magic work?)

Equations (What equations did you use to make the trick work?)

What Is Your Age? Multiplication, Addition, Division, and Subtraction

Say: **In this trick I will be able to guess your age correctly.**

THE PROPS

dark-colored marker

large piece of paper

THE TRICK

1. Give a volunteer the marker and put on your blindfold.

2. Say: **Write down your age and multiply it by 3.**

3. Say: **Add 6 to that number.**

4. Say: **Divide your answer by 3.**

5. Say: **Tell me your answer and I will tell you how old you are.**

6. In your head, subtract 2 from the number she gave you.

7. Say some magic words and announce your answer. It will be the volunteer's age. Honest!

THE MAGIC

This trick is another one where the volunteer does all the work for you. You just take the credit for the magic.

Why does this work?

In this trick, the person's age is multiplied by 3 and then divided by 3. This brings her back to her beginning number, which is her age!

Example:

Suppose the volunteer is 10 years old.

$10 \times 3 = 30$ (the volunteer multiples 10 by 3).

$30 + 6 = 36$ (the volunteer adds 6 to that answer).

$36 \div 3 = 12$ (the volunteer divides that answer by 3).

$12 - 2 = 10$ (you subtract 2 from that answer).

Instead of adding 6 in the trick, you can add any number that can be divided evenly by the number 3. You can use 9 and subtract 3 from the final answer because 9 divided by 3 equals 3. Or add 12 and subtract 4 from the final answer because 12 divided by 3 equals 4. If you add 15, what number would you subtract?

What Is Your Age? Multiplication, Addition, Division, and Subtraction

Name _____ Date _____

Now you try it:

1. Write your age on a piece of paper.
2. Multiply it by 3.
3. Add 6.
4. Divide the answer by 3.
5. Subtract 2. And here you are again, right back at your age!

Remember, if you want to change the trick, you can ask the volunteer to add any number that is divisible by 3. Instead of asking her to add 6, she can add 9 and then you subtract 3 instead of 2 (9 ÷ 3 = 3). Suppose you told her to add 18. What number would you subtract? 18 ÷ 3 = ?

How did you do?

Materials (What props did you use?)

Procedure (How did you do the trick?)

Conclusion (What makes the magic work?)

Equations (What equations did you use to make the trick work?)

Young or Old: Addition with Carrying and Subtraction with Borrowing

Say: **Here is another way I will be able to guess someone's age, no matter how young or old.**

THE PROPS

dark-colored marker

large piece of paper

small pad and pencil

THE TRICK

1. Put the pad and pencil in your pocket. Then give a volunteer a marker and turn your back.
2. Say: **Will you please write your age on the paper.**
3. Say: **Because there are 12 months in a year, would you please add the number 12 to your age.**
4. Say: **Because there are 7 days in a week and 52 weeks in a year, would you please add the number 752 to that answer.**
5. Say: **Now tell me your final answer.**
6. Say: **This is a complicated problem. You're making me work very hard.**

   While you are talking, take the pad and pencil out of your pocket and use it to subtract 64 from the number given to you.
7. Say some magic works and tell the volunteer the last two numbers of your answer. That will be his age. If the volunteer is under 10 years old, tell him just the final number in your answer.

THE MAGIC

Here is another trick in which the volunteer adds certain numbers to his age and you subtract them to get his age.

How does this work?

We are concerned only about the numbers that are added in the 10's and 1's column. The number in the 100's column will not affect our answer. After the volunteer writes his age, he adds 12 and 752. This makes a total of 6 in the 10's (1 and 5) column and two 2's for a total of 4 in the 1's columns. 6 in the 10's column and 4 in the 1's column make 64. The volunteer has added 64 to his age. When you subtract 64 from the last two digits, you will have his age. The last two digits gives you 46, which is the age of the volunteer.

Example:

Age: 46

```
   46        58        810
  +12      +752       -64
   58       810        746
```

Sounds so complicated, doesn't it, but it's really very simple when you know what you're doing!

Young or Old: Addition with Carrying and Subtraction with Borrowing

Name _____ Date _____

Now you try it:

1. Write down your age.

2. Add 12.

3. Add 752.

4. Subtract 64.

5. Are the last two numbers your age? Of course they are. Numbers never lie!

How did you do?

Materials (What props did you use?)

Procedure (How did you do the trick?)

Conclusion (What makes the magic work?)

Equations (What equations did you use to make the trick work?)

Magic Fingers: Trickery!

Say: **In this trick I will be able to tell which number is picked from eight written numbers.**

THE PROPS

small paper bag

pen or pencil for recording numbers

eight small pieces of paper (Tear two pieces of notebook paper into eight equal parts.)

THE TRICK

1. Call on eight different members of the audience to give you a two-digit number.
2. As they give you the numbers, write each on a separate piece of paper.
3. Fold the papers as tightly as you can and put them in a small paper bag.
3. Shake the bag and ask a volunteer to pick one folded paper from the bag.
4. Put the bag away.
5. Say: **Now my magic fingers will tell me which number is written on this paper.**
6. Take the paper from the volunteer. Close your eyes. Don't unfold the paper. Pretend you are thinking very hard.
7. Say some magic words and tell the audience which number is on the paper.
8. Ask the volunteer to open the paper and read the number. It will be the one you said. Take your bow.

THE MAGIC

This trick isn't magical, but it's a fun way to fool the audience.

Why does this work?

When you are given numbers, you pretend you are writing the numbers called out. In reality you write the first number you are given on all the papers! So, of course, you will know which number was picked from the bag because each paper will have the same number.

Magic Fingers: Trickery!

Name _____ Date _____

Now you try it:

This is a simple trick to do, but it would be a good idea to practice writing the numbers so no one will guess you are writing the same number over and over. You might want to hold one hand in front of the papers as you write so the audience can't see in which direction your pencil is moving.

1. Ask a friend to give you at least eight different numbers.
2. Pretend you are writing the numbers on small slips of paper while you write only the first number given on each paper.
3. Fold each paper tightly and put them in a small bag.
4. Ask someone to choose a folded paper from the bag. Hold the folded paper in your hands with your eyes closed and pretend to be thinking very hard.
5. Finally, say what the number is and have someone unfold the paper to read the number. It will be the one you said, of course!

How Did You Do?

Materials (What props did you use?)

Procedure (How did you do the trick?)

Conclusion (What makes the magic work?)

Changeover: Addition, Subtraction, Multiplication, and Division

Say: **In this trick you will pick a number and change it in five ways, but I will know what number you end up with.**

THE PROPS

dark-colored marker, large piece of paper

THE TRICK

1. Give the marker to a volunteer and put on your blindfold.
2. Say: **Pick a number and double it. That's change number 1.**
3. Say: **Now change it a second time by adding 9 to your answer.**
4. Say: **Now subtract 3 from your answer to change it a third time.**
5. Say: **The fourth change you will make is to divide the answer by 2.**
6. Say: **The fifth way you will change your number is to subtract the number you started with.**
7. Put your hands to your head as if you are concentrating very hard.
8. Say some magic words, then say: **After all the changes you made in your number you are left with the number 3.**

THE MAGIC

This is yet another trick where everything the volunteer does takes her to the number you have chosen, in this case a 3.

Why does this work?

When you double a number, then divide it by 2, you end up with the same number you started with. This is what the volunteer does in the first and fourth changes. The part of the trick that makes the magic is when you add the 9. When you add 9 and subtract 3 you end up with 6 (9 − 3 = 6). The 6 is in the number that you divide by 2 in the fourth change; 6 is added to 10 (6 ÷ 2 = 3). All that's left after all that work is the number 3. That is your final answer. Remember in the last step that you subtract the original number so there is nothing left of that number in the answer.

Example:

Start with the number 5.

First change: Double that number. 5 × 2 = 10.

Second change: Add 9 to that answer. 10 + 9 = 19.

Third change: Subtract 3 from that answer. 19 − 3 = 16.

Fourth change: Divide the answer by 2. 16 ÷ 2 = 8.

Fifth change: Subtract 5 (the original number). 8 − 5 = 3.

Changeover: Addition, Subtraction, Multiplication, and Division

Name _____ Date _____

Now you try it:

1. Write a number and double it.

2. Add 9.

3. Subtract 3.

4. Divide the number by 2.

5. Subtract the number you started with. Is the answer 3? Yes it is! You are quite a magician.

How did you do?

Materials (What props did you use?)

Procedure (How did you do the trick?)

Conclusion (What makes the magic work?)

Equations (What equations did you use to make the trick work?)

Lucky 63: Addition with Double-Digit Numbers

Say: **In this trick you will pick a number from 1 to 63, and I will be able to tell you which number you picked.**

THE PROPS

six number charts

(These can be found in the Appendix. Mount them on cardboard so the audience can see them.

There is no special order.)

THE TRICK

1. Turn your back, and ask a volunteer to pick a number from 1 to 63 and write it on a small piece of paper.
2. Say: **Give the paper to anyone in the audience to keep until I guess which number you picked.**
3. Turn back to the volunteer. Hold up the charts. Point to each box and say: **Is your number in this box?**
4. In your head or using paper and pencil, add the *top left-hand number* in each of the boxes that has the number.
5. Say some magic words, then announce the sum of the numbers you have just added.
6. Ask the person in the audience to read what number is on the paper he is holding. It will be the number you guessed. No kidding!

THE MAGIC

Here is a mind-boggling trick that uses plain addition to fool people. This trick will really impress your audience.

Why does this work?

The numbers are already arranged so that the trick will work. All you have to do is to add the top left-hand number of each box that holds the secret number. The sum of the top left-hand numbers will always give you the secret number.

Lucky 63: Addition with Double-Digit Numbers

Name _____ Date _____

Now you try it:

1. Pick a number from 1 to 63.

2. Add the top left-hand number in just the boxes that contain the number. Is the sum of your addition the number you picked? Of course it is!

Your teacher has the charts you will need for this trick. Please ask for copies.

How did you do?

Materials (What props did you use?)

Procedure (How did you do the trick?)

Conclusion (What makes the magic work?)

Equations (What equations did you use to make the trick work?)

Chapter VI
MULTIPLICATION MYSTERIES

✳ ✳ ✳ ✳ ✳ ✳ ✳ ✳ ✳ ✳ ✳

Teacher Notes

This chapter contains some interesting facts about the number 9 plus a few out-of-the-ordinary ways to multiply without too much strain on the brain!

Trick 1. Magic 9's or the Folded Finger

This is a simple way to learn the 9 times table or to use the number facts of the 9 times table without memorizing it!

Trick 2. More Multiplication Magic for 9

Here is another easy way to remember the 9 times table!

Trick 3. More About the Mysterious 9

Two more facts about the 9 times table:
• Adding the numbers in each product from the 9's table will give the sum of 9.
• Adding any or all of the products from the 9's table and then adding the digits in that sum will also give 9.
And one last trick: How to make 100 using four 9's!

Trick 4. Multiplication Magic for Times Tables 6 through 10

Here is a method for arriving at the answers to the multiplication tables from 6 through 10 using the fingers on both hands. There is also a cursory introduction to our base 10 number system.

✳ ✳ ✳ ✳ ✳ ✳ ✳ ✳ ✳ ✳ ✳

Teacher Script

Say you're taking a test and your mind goes blank. You need to know what 8 times 7 is, but you can't remember and the clock is ticking away.

Wouldn't it be good to have a way to figure out the answer without having to take the time to add 8 seven times? In fact wouldn't it be great to have a fast way to get the answers to the multiplication tables whenever you need them? That's exactly what you are going to learn. Using a simple finger trick, you will be able to get all the answers to the times table from the 6's table through the 9's table.

You also are about to find out some strange facts about the number 9.

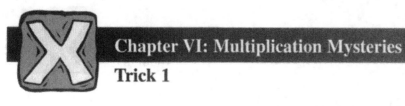

Magic 9's or the Folded Finger

Here is a magic way to learn the multiplication table for the number 9:

1. Put your hands in front of you with thumbs touching. In your mind, number your fingers from 1 to 10: 1 is your left-hand pinkie and 10 is your right-hand pinkie.

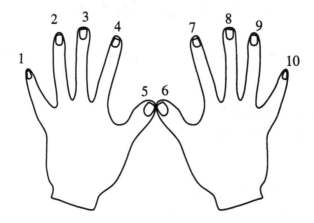

2. For 9 × 1, fold under number 1. There are 9 fingers still up because 9 × 1 = 9.

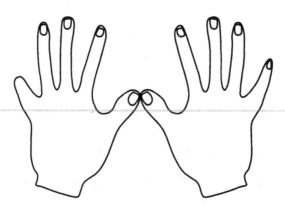

3. For 9×2, fold under finger number 2. There is 1 finger to the left of finger 2 and 8 fingers up to the right of it. That's because $9 \times 2 = 18$.

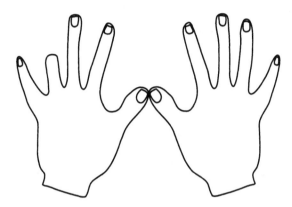

4. Try this with folding down finger 3. How many are to the left and how many to the right? 2 on the left and 7 on the right, right? $9 \times 3 = 27$.

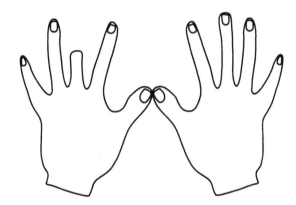

5. Do you see the pattern? Whichever finger you put under is the number you are multiplying by 9. The 10's part of the answer will always be to the left of the folded finger. The 1's part of the answer will be the number of fingers to the right of the folded finger.

More Multiplication Magic for 9

When your mind goes blank and you can't remember the 9 times table, here's another simple way to get the right answers. You just have to use simple addition and subtraction.

Example:

5×9

Take 1 from the 5 to make 4. The first number will be 4 ($5 - 1 = 4$).

Subtract 4 from 9 to get 5. The second number will be 5 ($9 - 4 = 5$).

$5 \times 9 = 45$

Does this work with all the numbers in the nine times table? Yes, it does.

Example:

7×9
1 from 7 is 6 ($7 - 1 = 6$), so 6 is the first number.
Subtract 6 from 9 to get 3 ($9 - 6 = 3$) for the second number.
So, 7×9 is 63.

Let's take one more example: 3×9
One less than 3 is 2 ($3 - 1 = 2$), so the first number is 2.
9 take away 2 is 7 ($9 - 2 = 7$), which is the second number.
9×3 equals 27.

Sorry, this doesn't work for any of the other times tables, only the mysterious 9!

MULTIPLICATION MYSTERIES Trick 3
Even More About the Mysterious 9

Here's another mysterious fact about the 9 times table. If you add the numbers in each product through 9 times 10, you end up with 9!

$9 \times 1 = 9$ $9 \times 6 = 54 (5 + 4 = 9)$

$9 \times 2 = 18 (1 + 8 = 9)$ $9 \times 7 = 63 (6 + 3 = 9)$

$9 \times 3 = 27 (2 + 7 = 9)$ $9 \times 8 = 72 (7 + 2 = 9)$

$9 \times 4 = 36 (3 + 6 = 9)$ $9 \times 9 = 81 (8 + 1 = 9)$

$9 \times 5 = 45 (4 + 5 = 9)$ $9 \times 10 = 90 (9 + 0 = 9)$

And here's more. If you add some or even all of the products from the 9's table, the digits in the answer will always add up to 9!

Examples:

$9 + 18 + 27 = 54$ and $5 + 4 = 9$

$18 + 27 + 36 + 45 + 54 + 63 + 72 + 81 + 90 = 486$ and $4 + 8 + 6 = 18$ and $1 + 8 = 9$

Interesting, isn't it, to play with the number 9? Maybe 9 is mysterious because it is the largest number in our system of numbers that can be written as one digit.

Here's one last trick with 9: Ask your friends if they know how to put four 9's together to make 100. They will probably not be able to do it, but you can. Simply write "99 $\frac{9}{9}$." This equals 100 because the fraction $\frac{9}{9}$ is the same as 1 and $99 + 1 = 100$!

Multiplication Magic for Times Tables 6 through 10

To do this trick, you must know your multiplication tables from the 1's through the 5's. These are the tables that are easy to learn and remember. Because you learned long ago how to count by 1's, 2's and 5's, you've known most of them forever.

Just as you did in the last trick, put your hands in front of you, only this time number them differently. Number both pinkies 6 and both thumbs 10. The fingers in between are 7, 8, and 9.

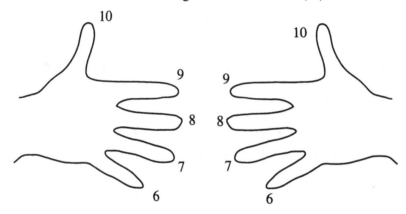

Put the tips of the fingers together of the numbers you want to multiply. For example, if you want to multiply 8 × 8, put both middle fingers together. Make sure your thumbs are on top and pinkies on the bottom just as they are in the picture.

To get the 10's part of your answer, count by 10 all the fingers below the touching fingers and the touching fingers too. This is the pinky side.

To get the 1's part of the answer, count the number of fingers on each hand above the touching fingers and multiply them. This is the thumb side.

So for 8 × 8, there are 6 fingers in all when you count the touching fingers and the fingers below them, making 60.

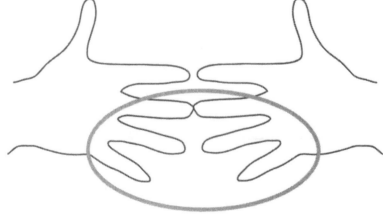

And there are 2 fingers on each hand above the touching fingers. $2 \times 2 = 4$.

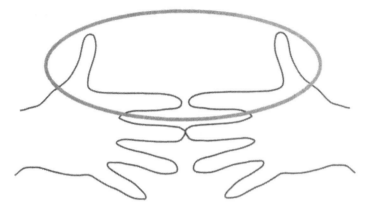

Then add your 10's and your 1's. $60 + 4 = 64$. So $8 \times 8 = 64$.

Let's try another example. How about 7×9? The second finger (7) of your left hand is touching the fourth finger of your right hand. There are 6 fingers counting the touching fingers and the fingers below them. That makes 60.

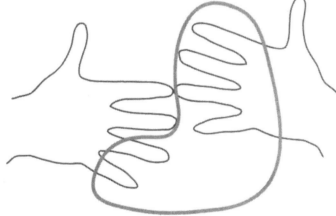

There are 3 on top on the left hand and 1 on top on the right hand. $3 \times 1 = 3$. $60 + 3 = 63$ and $7 \times 9 = 63$.

There is one tricky multiplication problem and that is 6×6. When you put your two pinkies together and count the 10's, there are only two! Because 6×6 equals 36, that is not the right number of 10's!

It all works out in the end because when you multiply the fingers on the left hand by the fingers on the right, you get 16 ($4 \times 4 = 16$).

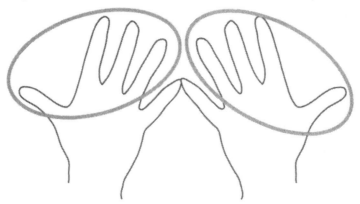

$16 + 20 = 36$ and $6 \times 6 = 36$. All's well that ends well.

After you practice this awhile, you will see how quick and easy it is to get the answers to multiplication questions. It's even faster than using a calculator plus it's very handy for taking tests when you're not allowed to use a calculator.

Why does this work?

Actually, I'm not quite sure why this method of multiplication works. I think it may work because our number system is based on the number 10 and we are working with 10 fingers. A number system based on the number 10 means that no matter how large a number is, it can have only 10 different symbols or digits: 1, 2, 3, 4, 5, 6, 7, 8, 9, 0. After we get to the number 9, we start all over again with 1 and 0.

It's fun to see how numbers would work if they were in a system based on another number like 6. Then there would be only 6 symbols or digits that could be used to make numbers. You would count, 1, 2, 3, 4, 5, 6, 11, 12, 13, 14, 15, 16, 21, and so on.

Suppose the number system were based on the number 4? How would you count?

Multiplication Magic for Times Tables 6 through 10

Name _____ Date _____

Now you try it:

1. Pick any two numbers.
2. Hold your hands just as they are shown in the illustrations with thumbs on top and pinkies on the bottom.
3. Pick the two numbers you want to multiply.
4. Put those two fingers together.
5. Count the 10's from the pinkies up, including the touching fingers.
6. Count the 1's by multiplying the top fingers on one hand by the top fingers on the other hand.
7. Did you end up with the right answer? Of course you did. This works every time.

Remember: The fingers on both hands are numbered the same, from 6 to 10, pinkies to thumbs.

How did you do?

Materials (What props did you use?)

Procedure (How did you do the trick?)

Conclusion (What makes the magic work?)

Equations (What equations did you use to make the trick work?)

Chapter VII
GAMES

✳ ✳ ✳ ✳ ✳ ✳ ✳ ✳ ✳ ✳

Teacher Notes

Probably from the time of the first schoolrooms, teachers have used games to help students learn many subjects. Kids love to play games. Sometimes the best learning takes place when students are unaware that they're learning and are just having a good time.

This chapter includes a few games designed for the whole class. They involve practice in mental computation and can serve as fillers for those times when you have a few extra minutes before an activity or before dismissal.

There are also directions for several games that can be played in small groups. These games strengthen basic skills by providing practice in performing math functions quickly. They can be used as a free time activity or as an opening or closing to a math lesson.

Before instructing the students on how to play the games, remind them that they must decide in a fair way who gets the first turn. There are many ways to choose who goes first in a game. The person throwing the highest or lowest number on a die can go first. The players can flip a coin to see who will go first. The players can count buttons on their clothing, and whoever has the most or the fewest buttons goes first. Maybe the oldest person or the youngest person can begin, or the person with the smallest shoe size can go first. Anything goes, as long as it's fair.

Pig in the Pokey

The first game, Pig in the Pokey, is similar to the popular and well-loved spelling game called Hangman, only in a math version. Also, a pig in jail is drawn instead of a man being hung.

WHAT YOU WILL NEED
Chalkboard and chalk
Students seated or standing in a configuration so each is in line for a turn

OBJECT OF THE GAME
To avoid putting the pig in the pokey (jail) for as long as possible

HOW TO PLAY
1. Give the students, in turn, a math problem to solve mentally.
2. Draw a part of the picture of a pig in jail every time an incorrect answer is given. Draw the bars of the cell last. (A student also could draw the pig in jail.) When the figure is complete, the game is over.

One of the advantages of this game is that it can be used to practice any math understanding you are teaching at the time. You can practice measurement by calling out a measure and asking the student to answer with an equivalent. You can use the times tables or simple division problems or word problems.

An enjoyable way to play is to mix all sorts of math computations together so students don't know what kind of question they will get.

Around the World

Each player tries to stay in the game as long as possible by correctly adding 25 to a number called out by the preceding player.

Before playing this game, review with the students that the easiest way to add 25 to another number is to first add 2 to the 10's column and then count up 5. Each time the game is played, urge students to improve the time it takes for everyone to respond. Recording the response time of the class can be the basis of several lessons in making bar and line graphs.

After you have played this game for a period of time, change 25 to a more challenging number, or use the game for subtraction or multiplication practice.

WHAT YOU WILL NEED

Students sitting or standing in an arrangement where they will all get a turn in sequence

OBJECT OF THE GAME

To stay in the game by quickly and correctly adding 25 to any number from 1 to 100 given by the preceding player

HOW TO PLAY

1. Have students sit or stand in any arrangement where each will get a turn.
2. Call out a number from 1 to 100 to the first person.
3. After adding 25 to that number correctly, the student calls out a number to the next person in line as quickly as possible. If the answer is incorrect, the next student in line uses the same number.

Nim

Nim is a game of logic where each player tries to make his opponent pick up the last object from the table.

WHAT YOU WILL NEED

2 players

15 objects (pieces of candy, coins, buttons, or other small objects)

OBJECT OF THE GAME

To make your opponent pick up the last object from the table

HOW TO PLAY

1. Lay out 15 objects in a row on a table.
2. Take turns picking up from one to three objects from the table. The winner is the one who makes the opponent pick up the last object from the table.

Here's how to always win at the game of Nim. When you take your objects from the table, always try to leave the following number of objects: 13, 9, 5, or 1. These numbers are easy to remember because they are all 4 numbers apart and they are all odd. Why do you think this winning trick always works? Try it with a partner and find out for yourself:

1. Lay out 15 objects.
2. You take away 2 to leave 13.
3. Your opponent must take away 1 to 3 objects. She leaves 12 or 11 or 10.
4. You take away 1 or 2 or 3 to leave 9.
5. Again she must take away from 1 to 3 and leave either 8 or 7 or 6.
6. You take away 1 or 2 or 3 to leave 5.
7. She takes away from 1 to 3 to leave 4 or 3 or 2.
8. You take away either 3 or 2 or 1 to leave one object that she must take.
9. You win!

You will always win if you remember the magic numbers of 13, 9, 5, 1. If your opponent knows the magic numbers, too, try to go first because the person who goes first will win!

Now here's a puzzler: If you play the game of Nim with 21 objects, can you figure out what the magic numbers are that you should use so you always win? How about with 25?

Bulls and Cows

This next game is a game of logic where a player has to guess a number that another player has chosen. Normally this game is played by two players, but it can be played by more. In fact, the entire class can play this game together. If several people play, each player takes turns guessing at the number.

WHAT YOU WILL NEED

2 or more players

paper and pencil

OBJECT OF THE GAME

To guess a number that someone has chosen

HOW TO PLAY

1. The first player is the farmer. The farmer thinks of a four-digit number (for example, 3245).
2. The other players in turn guess by saying any four-digit number.
3. The farmer tells how close the guess is by saying how many bulls and cows there are.

   A *bull* means that the player has guessed a *correct digit in the correct position*. A *cow* means that the player has guessed a *correct digit, but it is in the wrong position*.
4. The players keep guessing until the mystery number is identified. The players should use the paper to record all guesses and the number of bulls and cows in each guess.
5. The player who guesses the correct number gets to be the farmer and choose the next number.

   Example:

   1847 is the original number.

   Guesses:

   3416   2 cows (two right digits in the wrong position)

   7834   2 cows, 1 bull (three correct digits and one, the 8, is in
   the right position)

   2847   3 bulls (three numbers in the right position)

   2841   2 bulls, 1 cow (two numbers in the right position and one
   correct digit in the wrong position)

   1847   Correct!

War

The next game is one that students probably have played many times. Two different and more challenging ways to play the game are presented.

WHAT YOU WILL NEED

2 decks of cards using just the numbered cards, which are worth their printed number in points, and the aces, which are worth one point

OBJECT OF THE GAME

To capture all the cards in both decks or end up with the most cards in a certain amount of time

Variation: Addition War
HOW TO PLAY

1. Each player starts out with a deck of shuffled cards with all kings, queens, and jacks discarded. Each card is worth its printed number with the ace worth 1 point.
2. Both players lay out two cards and add the numbers on them together.
3. Whichever player has the greater sum and names that sum correctly wins all four cards, which are put on the bottom of the cards he is holding.
4. If the player does not name the sum correctly on the first try, no one wins that hand. Instead the players put down two more cards and add all four of their cards. Whoever has and names the correct higher sum wins all eight cards.
5. If the sum for both players is the same, they put down two more cards. Whoever has and names the correct higher sum takes all the cards.
6. Play continues in this way until one player wins by getting all the cards. The winner also can be the player who has the most cards after a specified period of time.

Variation: Multiplication War
HOW TO PLAY

Play Multiplication War the same way as Addition War except multiply the two numbers instead of adding them. The person with the highest product wins the deal if he has done the multiplication correctly.

One Hundred and One

This dice game involves creative thinking, probability, addition, and subtraction.

WHAT YOU WILL NEED

1 die

2 or more players

OBJECT OF THE GAME

To reach a score of 101 by totaling the numbers thrown on the die

HOW TO PLAY

1. The first player tosses the die and receives as a score whatever number she has thrown.
2. The player can continue to throw as long as she wishes and total the numbers thrown. However, if she throws a 1, her turn ends and she must subtract whatever her score was for that turn. She can choose to stop rolling at any time and pass the die to the next person.
3. Scores are recorded for each turn and not added to the player's total score until the player's turn has ended.
4. The first player to reach 101 is the winner.

Fill Up the Box

This is another game in which students have to think logically and use their number sense.

WHAT YOU WILL NEED

sheet of paper with a box of 9 squares numbered from 1 to 9

9 playing pieces (beans or rocks or candies or whatever is handy)

2 dice

paper and pencil for recording scores

OBJECT OF THE GAME

To cover as many numbers as possible in the box and end up with the lowest score

HOW TO PLAY

1. Each player in turn throws the dice and adds the numbers thrown.
2. The player must decide which numbered squares to cover on the box.
3. The player can choose any combination of the number rolled. For instance, if a 9 was rolled, the player could cover the 9, or he could cover a 6 and a 3, or he could cover a 5 and a 4. He can choose to cover only numbers that do not have a marker on them.
4. When the highest ones (7, 8, 9) have been covered, the player may choose to throw only one die at a time.
5. The player's turn ends when he throws a number that he cannot use to fill up the box.
6. All numbers that are uncovered are added, and that is the player's score.
7. After all the players have had their turn, the one with the lowest score is the winner.

This page and the following five pages are ready to be posted on oak-tag to be used in Chapter V, Trick 6. There is no special order for posting.

1	3	5	7
9	11	13	15
17	19	21	23
25	27	29	31
33	35	37	39
41	43	45	47
49	51	53	55
57	59	61	63

2	3	6	7
10	11	14	15
18	19	22	23
26	27	30	31
34	35	38	39
42	43	46	47
50	51	54	55
58	59	62	63

4	5	6	7
12	13	14	15
20	21	22	23
28	29	30	31
36	37	38	39
44	45	46	47
52	53	54	55
60	61	62	63

8	9	10	11
12	13	14	15
24	25	26	27
28	29	30	31
40	41	42	43
44	45	46	47
56	57	58	59
60	61	62	63

16	17	18	19
20	21	22	23
24	25	26	27
28	29	30	31
48	49	50	51
52	53	54	55
56	57	58	59
60	61	62	63

32	33	34	35
36	37	38	39
40	41	42	43
44	45	46	47
48	49	50	51
52	53	54	55
56	57	58	59
60	61	62	63

INDEX: Magic Tricks Indexed According to Math Skills

Printed in the USA
CPSIA information can be obtained
at www.ICGtesting.com
LVHW080722170724
785510LV00007B/267